HISTORY & GEOGRAPHY 510

THE UNITED STATES OF AMERICA

S0-CJN-195

Author:
Theresa Buskey, J.D.

Editor:
Alan Christopherson, M.S.

Media Credits:
Page 3, 68: © Stocktrek Images, Thinkstock; **5:** © Willard, iStock, Thinkstock; **6:** © Peter Dennis, Thinkstock; **10, 12, 15, 16, 20, 54:** © Photos.com, Thinkstock; **11:** © William Sherman, iStock, Thinkstock; **14:** © flySnow, iStock, Thinkstock; **18:** © Natalia Bratslavsky, iStock, Thinkstock; **19:** © giftlegacy, iStock, Thinkstock; **19, 35:** © Jupiter Images, liquidlibrary, Thinkstock; **23:** © Adam Parent, iStock, Thinkstock; **26:** © Bitter, iStock, Thinkstock; © Elizabeth Fisher, iStock, Thinkstock; **33:** © mirecca, iStock, Thinkstock; **36:** E.B. & E.C. Kellogg (Firm), U. S. Library of Congress; **37:** Hammatt Billings; **40:** © Jupiterimages, Photos.com, Thinkstock; **41:** © Tobias Bischof, iStock, Thinkstock; **42:** © Brand X Pictures, Thinkstock; **44:** William Allen Rogers, Granger Collection; **45:** Bain News Service, U. S. Library of Congress; **53:** Master Sgt. Cecilio Ricardo, U.S. Air Force; **55:** U.S. Air Force; **56:** Charles Levy, National Archives and Records Administration; **59:** Republic of China; **60:** © U.S. Navy; **61:** Department of Defense, National Archives and Records Administration; **63:** National Archives and Records Administration; **64:** Max Smith; **65:** U.S. Air Force; **67:** Robert J. Fisch.

All maps in this book © Map Resources, unless otherwise stated.

Alpha Omega
PUBLICATIONS

804 N. 2nd Ave. E.
Rock Rapids, IA 51246-1759

THE UNITED STATES OF AMERICA

This **LIFEPAC®** is a review of the history of the United States of America. This **LIFEPAC** will retell the most important points you have studied over the last year. It will help you to see all of American history in one sweep.

Because this is a review, it does not give many details or explanations. If you need more detailed information, refer to the original LIFEPAC, an encyclopedia, or reliable online resources. The same is true of any words you do not recognize. Look them up in a dictionary or online

Objective

Read this objective. The objective tells you what you should be able to do when you have successfully completed this LIFEPAC.

- When you have finished this LIFEPAC, you should be able to give a general overview of American history, recognizing important people, inventions, wars, and events.

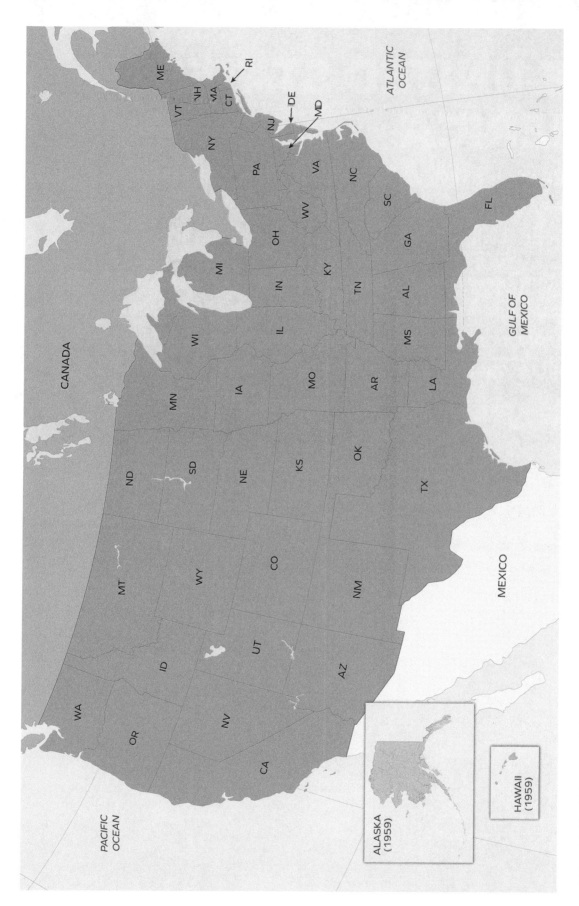

ATLANTIC OCEAN

GULF OF MEXICO

CANADA

MEXICO

PACIFIC OCEAN

ME
NH
MA
VT
CT
RI
NY
NJ
DE
MD
PA
VA
WV
NC
SC
FL
GA
OH
KY
TN
AL
IN
IL
MS
MI
WI
MO
AR
LA
MN
IA
ND
SD
NE
KS
OK
TX
MT
WY
CO
NM
UT
ID
AZ
WA
NV
OR
CA

ALASKA (1959)

HAWAII (1959)

| The United States of America

1. BEGINNING AMERICA (UNTIL 1830)

This section will review the origins of the United States. It will discuss the European explorers who mapped and named our land. It will also retell the stories of how the original thirteen colonies were founded.

This section will then discuss why Britain and the colonies came into conflict. This conflict over taxes and laws led the American colonists to declare their independence and create the nation called the United States of America.

Objective

Review the objective. When you have finished this section, you should be able to:

- Give a general overview of American history, recognizing important people, inventions, wars, and events.

Origins of the United States

Discovery of North America. North America was first settled by people from Asia who crossed the Bering Sea long before the Europeans began to explore. These people were the ancestors of the many Native Americans who still live here today.

The first Europeans to come to America were Vikings from Greenland. Led by Leif Ericson, the Vikings sailed to Canada around A.D. 1000. They were not able to colonize the land, and the story of their discovery never reached most of Europe.

In the 1400s, Europeans began to explore and map the world. They were looking for an all-water route to Asia because they wanted spices which were very popular and profitable in Europe. By 1498 Portugal had found the first route by going around Africa. The idea came from Henry the Navigator, a prince of Portugal, who set up a school to train sailors in the 1400s.

Christopher Columbus, an Italian sea captain, believed he could reach Asia by sailing west, around the world. He thought Asia was much closer to Europe than it really is, and he did not know America was in the way. He convinced the rulers of Spain, King Ferdinand and Queen Isabella, to sponsor his voyage.

Columbus sailed in 1492 with three ships: the *Niña*, the *Pinta*, and the *Santa Maria*. He landed that year on an island in the "West Indies" (so named to tell them from the East Indies in Asia). Columbus named the island San Salvador. He believed he had landed in Asia, but he could not find any wealthy cities and finally returned to Spain.

He went to America three more times. He founded the very first European colony in America, Isabela, on the island of Hispaniola. He never did learn the truth, that he had found the New World and not Asia.

| Christopher Columbus planned to reach Asia by sailing west, around the world.

Spanish explorers. Spain sent men to colonize and conquer the lands Columbus had found. *Conquistadors* began to map the land as they hunted for gold. Slowly, they learned more about the land and realized it was not Asia. This was confirmed when Spain sponsored Magellan on the first voyage around the world in 1519. Only one of his five ships survived the voyage, and Magellan was killed in the Philippines. However, the voyage proved that the world was a sphere and America was far from Asia.

Other Spanish explorers were the first Europeans to reach parts of what is now the United States. Ponce de León explored and named Florida while looking for the fountain of youth. Hernando de Soto found the Mississippi River when he investigated the land north and west of Florida. Francisco Coronado went searching for seven cities of gold north of Mexico. Instead, he found the Grand Canyon and land that would one day be Arizona, New Mexico, and Texas. Spain also founded the first colony in the U.S., the city of St. Augustine in Florida.

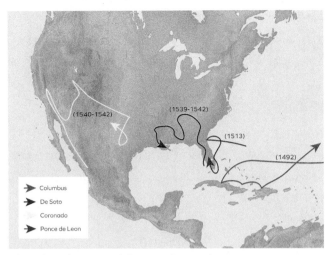

| Columbus and Spanish explorers

New France. The French king wanted gold and to find the Northwest Passage through North America to Asia. In about 1530, he sent Jacques Cartier to explore the gulf west of the Grand Banks, the fishing area near Canada. Cartier found and named the St. Lawrence River. He explored it as far as what is now Montreal.

Samuel de Champlain started the first French colony in 1608 at Quebec. He also explored the rest of the St. Lawrence, parts of Lake Ontario, Lake Huron, and upstate New York where he found the large lake now called Lake Champlain. He became known as the "father of New France" for his work.

New France spread as the colonists searched for new areas to trade for furs. Furs were very valuable in Europe, and the French traded with the Indians for them. They set up forts along the rivers to protect their country, holding large amounts of land with very few people.

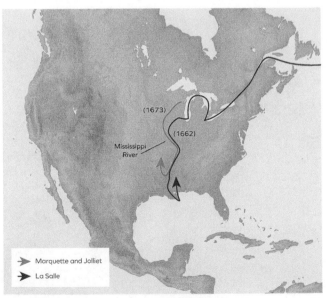

| French explorers

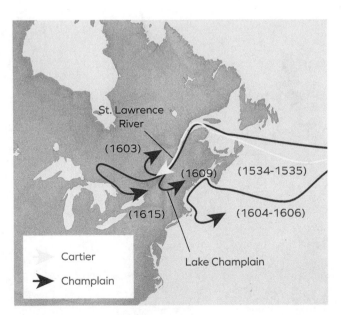

After spreading along the St. Lawrence and the Great Lakes, New France pushed south along the Mississippi River. Two Frenchmen, Jacques Marquette and Louis Jolliet, explored the river as far south as Arkansas in 1673. Sieur de La Salle followed it to its mouth on the Gulf of Mexico in 1682. He claimed all of the land drained by the river for France, all of the center part of what is now the U.S.

New Netherlands. In 1609 Henry Hudson explored the Hudson River in New York for the Dutch. The Dutch West India Company started a colony there to farm and trade for furs. They bought Manhattan Island and started a city there. The British took over the colony in 1664 and renamed it New York.

English exploration. Several English explorers also made claims for their nation. John Cabot found the Grand Banks and explored along the northeast coast of the continent soon after Columbus sailed. Beginning in 1577, Sir Francis Drake explored the coast of California on a trip he made around the world, raiding Spanish towns. Henry Hudson sailed for

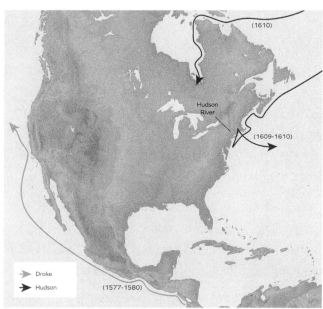

| Dutch and English explorers

England and explored northern Canada looking for the Northwest Passage in 1610. Hudson Bay, where he was left behind by his men, was named after him. This gave England a claim to the U.S. east coast and Canada around the borders of New France.

Name the explorer.

1.1 Led the first voyage around the world: _____

1.2 Explored and named the St. Lawrence River: _____

1.3 Explored New York for the Netherlands and northern Canada for England:

_____

1.4 Discovered America by sailing west to reach Asia for Spain:

_____

1.5 First European to reach America, Viking: _____

1.6 Found the Grand Banks, explored the northeast coast for England:

_____

1.7 Founded Quebec, explored Lakes Ontario and Huron as well as northern New York:

_____

1.8 Explored and named Florida while looking for the fountain of youth:

_____

1.9 Set up a school of navigation and organized Portugal's discovery of an all-water

route to Asia around Africa: _____

1.10 Explored north and west of Florida, discovered the Mississippi River:

_____

1.11 Raided Spanish towns and explored the coast of California on a trip around the world:

_____

1.12 Explored Texas, Arizona, and New Mexico looking for cities of gold:

_____

1.13 Explored the Mississippi River from the north as far as Arkansas:

_____

1.14 Claimed all of the land drained by the Mississippi for France after he followed the

river to its mouth: _____

Complete these sentences.

1.15 Europeans wanted to reach Asia to trade for _____ .

1.16 The product the French wanted in New France was _____ .

1.17 Europeans wanted to find a way through or around North America called the

_____ to reach Asia.

1.18 New France spread along the St. Lawrence River, the _____ Lakes,

and the _____ River.

English colonies. The United States was created by the thirteen original colonies. These were all separate colonies of Great Britain. They were divided into three sections: New England, the Middle Colonies, and the Southern Colonies.

New England included four colonies. Pilgrim Separatists settled Plymouth in Massachusetts in 1620. Their ship, the *Mayflower*, was supposed to go to Virginia, but landed at Cape Cod by mistake. Massachusetts was legally founded by Puritans who came to escape religious persecution. Rhode Island was founded by Roger Williams who fled from Massachusetts in 1636. His colony was the first to have full freedom of religion. Connecticut was founded in 1636 by Thomas Hooker, a Massachusetts pastor who believed non-Puritans should be allowed to vote. New Hampshire was settled by people leaving Massachusetts.

| The Pilgrims settled Plymouth in present-day Massachusetts.

There were four Middle Colonies. New York began as New Netherlands, started by the Dutch West India Company. The Duke of York took over the colony for England in 1664. The Duke gave New Jersey to two of his friends in 1664. They organized a colony which they sold to the Quakers as a refuge. Pennsylvania was given to William Penn, a wealthy Quaker, by Charles II to pay a debt. Penn formed a fast-growing colony by offering cheap land, religious freedom, and fair government. Delaware was given to William Penn by the Duke of York and eventually became a separate colony from Pennsylvania.

There were five colonies in the South. Virginia was the very first colony, founded by the Virginia Company of London at Jamestown in 1607. It developed a plantation system using slaves to grow tobacco. That system spread all over the South using different crops. Maryland was founded by Lord Baltimore as a refuge for Catholics in 1634. North Carolina was the northern part of the land given to eight friends of Charles II in 1663. It was settled by farmers from Virginia. South Carolina (the southern part) was settled by planters from the West Indies, who grew rice and indigo. Georgia was started in 1733 by a group under James Oglethorpe as a place for debtors to work off their debts.

French and Indian War. Britain and France fought several wars during the 1600s and 1700s. The biggest war in North America was the French and Indian War (1754-1763). George Washington fought in the war as an aide to a British general. The British finally won the war by capturing key forts in New France, especially Quebec in 1759. When the war ended, France gave up all of its land in America. Britain owned all of Canada and all of the United States east of the Mississippi River.

Conflicts with Britain. The American Revolution began after the French and Indian War. Britain was deeply in debt. Its government decided to tax the American colonies and control them for the very first time. Before the war, the Americans had been left to run their own governments and trade. The only taxes they paid were passed by their own colonial assemblies.

Beginning in 1763, there were a series of British actions and American reactions that brought the two sides into conflict. The Proclamation of 1763 ordered the colonists not to settle west of the Appalachian Mountains. They ignored it.

The Stamp Act ordered the colonists to pay for a stamp on all important papers in 1765. Nine of the colonies met at the Stamp Act Congress, the first all-colony assembly. Americans boycotted British goods, and mobs attacked the stamp sellers. The tax was ended quickly, but in the Declaratory Act, Parliament said it had the right to control the colonies.

| Some Native Americans fought for the British, and others fought for the French.

The Townshend Acts taxed goods like tea, glass, and lead coming from Britain. The Americans boycotted again, and the taxes were ended except for the tax on tea.

The East India Company was given a monopoly on selling tea to the colonies in 1773. The Americans refused to accept the taxed tea. At the Boston Tea Party, the tea was thrown into the harbor. The British government reacted with the Intolerable Acts which closed Boston Harbor, put the city under military rule, and ended many of the freedoms of the people in Massachusetts. The First Continental Congress met in 1774 to protest the Intolerable Acts.

The military governor of Massachusetts sent troops to Lexington and Concord in 1775 to destroy military supplies and capture the colonial leaders. They were met at Lexington by the colonial militia, and shots were fired, beginning the War for Independence. More shooting occurred at Concord, and the British were fired upon by the militia all the way back to Boston.

The militia and the British fought again at the Battle of Bunker Hill a couple of months later. The Americans fortified the hill outside Boston, and the British troops attacked straight up the hill. The Americans drove them back twice but had to retreat when they ran out of gunpowder.

Second Continental Congress. The Second Continental Congress met in May of 1775. They appointed George Washington as commander of the army around Boston. They voted for independence on July 2, 1776. Thomas Jefferson wrote the Declaration of Independence to explain the decision. It was accepted on July 4, 1776, and that became the date we say the United States was born.

| The Sons of Liberty, dressed as Mohawk Indians, pour tea into Boston harbor.

Name the colony.

1.19 _____ Founded by Thomas Hooker

1.20 _____ Founded by eight friends of Charles II, settlers from West Indies set up plantations for indigo and rice

1.21 _____ The Pilgrims were there first, but the Puritans followed

1.22 _____ James Oglethorpe wanted to help debtors

1.23 _____ Jamestown was the first settlement, tobacco became its crop

1.24 _____ Founded by eight friends of Charles II, settlers were small farmers from Virginia

1.25 _____ Founded by Roger Williams with full freedom of religion

1.26 _____ Two colonies started by William Penn

_____

1.27 _____ Founded by Lord Baltimore as a refuge for Catholics

1.28 _____ Duke of York gave it to two friends who sold it to the Quakers as a refuge for their people

1.29 _____ New Netherlands, taken over by the Duke of York in 1664

➡️ **Name the law, event, or item.**

1.30 _____ War just before the American Revolution, gave the British control all the land east of the Mississippi

1.31 _____ Laws that closed Boston Harbor and ended many of the colony's freedoms

1.32 _____ Ordered the colonists not to settle west of the Appalachians

1.33 _____ Tea was thrown into the harbor to protest the tax

1.34 _____ Congress that appointed Washington as the army commander and voted for independence

1.35 _____ First all-colony assembly

1.36 _____ Taxes on tea, lead, glass, and other products from Britain

1.37 _____ Said parliament had the right to control the colonies

1.38 _____ Battle that began the Revolutionary War

1.39 _____ Congress that met to respond to the Intolerable Acts

1.40 _____ Tax on all important papers

1.41 _____ British were driven back twice off a hill held by the Americans outside Boston

1.42 _____ Written by Thomas Jefferson, explained the decision for independence

A New Nation

Early problems. The British had some advantages in their war with the colonists. Britain had an army and navy, more money, and better organization. However, they were thousands of miles from Britain. Orders could take months to reach an officer in America. They also had to conquer a huge wilderness. Moreover, their enemies were clever, determined men like George Washington.

The American Army, under the command of Washington, surrounded the British in Boston after Lexington. A group of patriots under Ethan Allen captured Fort Ticonderoga on Lake Champlain and sent the fort's cannons to Washington. He set the cannons up around Boston in early 1776. That forced the British to leave.

| Minutemen were colonial soldiers who could be ready to fight in a minute's notice.

The British Army then took New York City, defeating Washington at the Battle of Long Island in July of 1776. The Americans camped in New Jersey for the winter. On Christmas night, Washington crossed the Delaware River and surprised an army of Hessians (German soldiers fighting for Britain) at Trenton. Washington won that battle and another at Princeton soon after. The double victories gave the Americans hope and led men to join the army.

Turning point. A British Army came down Lake Champlain in 1777, retaking Ticonderoga. It was met by American militia and an army under the command of Horatio Gates and Benedict Arnold. The entire British Army was captured at Saratoga. After that victory, France and America signed a treaty of alliance in 1778.

The British Army at New York City, in the meantime, marched out and captured Philadelphia. Washington was unable to stop them, but his army was not captured. The Americans spent a cold, miserable, hungry winter at nearby Valley Forge. Baron von Steuben used the time to drill the men and make them into a better army.

Victory. The British were supplying the Indians in the west and encouraging them to attack American settlers. George Rogers Clark stopped that in 1778. He took some frontiersmen and captured the British forts in the northwest.

General Benedict Arnold, a hero at Saratoga, betrayed his country in 1780. He tried to sell the British an American fort in New York. The man carrying messages to the British for him was caught, and Arnold fled to the British. His name is used in America to describe a traitor.

The British had some temporary success in the south in 1779-1780. They captured Georgia and South Carolina. They were stopped, however, at King's Mountain when they tried to invade North Carolina.

Washington sent Nathanael Greene to drive out the British in the south. Greene succeeded by running them in circles. The British chased him, caught up to him, and lost men defeating him. Then, Greene and his men escaped and started over again. The British ran low on supplies and men. They gave up and withdrew from most of the south by the end of 1781.

| Cornwallis surrendered at Yorktown.

That same year, the British Army under Lord Cornwallis camped at Yorktown on Chesapeake Bay, waiting to be picked up and moved to New York. Washington's army and a French Army trapped Cornwallis there. The French Navy stopped the British Navy from reaching them. Cornwallis's entire army surrendered. It was the last important battle of the war.

The Treaty of Paris, which ended the war, was not signed until 1783. In the treaty, Britain accepted that America was independent and gave it all of the land between Canada and Florida east of the Mississippi River.

Life in America. After the Revolution, most people in America were farmers. The farms in the north were usually small, growing enough food for one family. In New England, the poor soil forced men to use the sea to make money for their families. Shipbuilding, fishing, and whaling were all large industries in New England. Trade was also important, both there and in the Middle States.

The first American factories of the Industrial Revolution were built in New England. Samuel Slater memorized the plans for the British cloth-making machines and came to America in disguise. He started the first American cloth factory in Connecticut in 1791. Eli Whitney started a factory using interchangeable parts to make guns, which sped up building them and made them easy to repair.

People on the frontier were mainly farmers. They were usually poor, strong, independent people who did not trust governments, banks, or Indians. They had to make most of the things they needed. There were few towns and places to buy things. Their pastor was often a circuit rider who visited occasionally.

The south was also mainly filled with farmers. Some of them were plantation owners who had lots of money, fine homes, many expensive things, and good educations. They invested their money in land and slaves, not factories. There were some small family farms also where people lived like the rest of the nation, working hard.

| Eli Whitney started a factory that produced interchangeable gun parts and later invented the cotton gin.

In 1793, Eli Whitney invented a machine to clean cotton called the cotton gin. The new cloth factories needed cotton, but it had been too expensive to clean before his invention. Southern farmers began to grow more cotton after that. They also began to depend more on their slaves. Southern slave owners were determined to keep slavery, even as most of the northern states ended it after the Revolution.

The slave trade was part of the triangle trade with Africa. Rum was taken to Africa and traded for slaves. The slaves were packed into crowded ships in chains for the Middle Passage, the trip to the Americas. In the West Indies, the slaves were traded for molasses which was sold in America or Britain where the ships picked up more rum. The trade in slaves was outlawed in America after 1808.

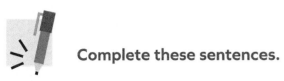

Complete these sentences.

1.43 The Americans twice captured a British Army at _____ and at _____ .

1.44 The cannons that drove the British out of Boston came from Fort _____ .

1.45 The American Army spent a cold, miserable winter at _____ near Philadelphia while Baron _____ drilled them.

1.46 _____ drove the British out of the south in 1780-1781, losing the battles.

1.47 _____ was a hero at Saratoga who became a traitor.

1.48 Cornwallis was trapped at Yorktown by the French Navy, an American Army under _____ , and a French Army.

1.49 Washington won a great victory at _____ after crossing the Delaware River on Christmas night and surprising the _____ .

1.50 France became a U.S. ally after the victory at _____ .

1.51 The Treaty of Paris gave the U.S. all the land between Canada and Florida east of the _____ .

1.52 _____ captured important forts in the west.

1.53 After the Revolution, most people in America were _____ .

1.54 Eli Whitney invented the _____ and built a gun factory that used _____ .

1.55 The first cloth factory in America was built by _____ .

1.56 New England had important industries in _____ , _____ and _____ .

1.57 The triangle trade brought _____ to Africa, _____ to the West Indies (the _____ Passage), and _____ to America or Britain.

1.58   Rich plantation owners in the south spent their money on _____

and _____ , not factories.

Articles of Confederation. The Second Continental Congress wrote a document for the U.S. called the Articles of Confederation. There was no president, and there were no federal courts. Congress could not tax or control trade. This created problems.

The Confederation Congress passed two important laws. The Land Ordinance of 1785 divided the land in the Northwest Territory into sections that were sold to pay off the national debt. The Northwest Ordinance of 1787 promised that when a territory had 60,000 people it could be added to the Union as a new state.

Constitutional Convention. The leaders of the nation met at Independence Hall in Philadelphia in the summer of 1787 to make a better government. They wrote the Constitution of the United States which we still use today. James Madison put in so many important ideas that he is called "the father of the Constitution."

The delegates made many compromises. The most important was the Great Compromise. It divided Congress into two parts. Each state had the same number of votes in the Senate, but in the House of Representatives states with more people had more votes.

The Constitution divided the power of the government into three parts: executive (president), legislative (congress), and judicial (courts). Each part or branch had some power over the others. This was to keep any one part from getting too powerful. Also, Amendments could be added to the Constitution if two-thirds of the states agreed.

| Independence Hall

Ratification. Two-thirds of the states (nine out of thirteen) had to ratify the Constitution for it to become law. People who supported the Constitution were called Federalists, those who opposed it were Anti-Federalists. Eventually, all of the states approved it, and the new government was elected in 1789.

Bill of Rights. The Anti-Federalist Party had one good argument, that the Constitution did not protect people's freedom. The first Congress fixed that by adding the first ten Amendments, the Bill of Rights. These Amendments protect freedom of religion, freedom of speech, the right to a fair trial, and many other important rights.

| Powers split between the legislative, judicial, and executive branches ensured that no one branch could take over the others.

New government. George Washington was the first president. His leadership made people trust the office. His service also earned him the title "father of his country." The four men he chose to work with him and advise him formed the president's cabinet. Thomas Jefferson was the first Secretary of State and Alexander Hamilton the first Secretary of the Treasury.

Hamilton wanted the new government to pay all of its debts and the debts of the states for the war. Many of the southern states had paid their own debts and did not want this. However, they agreed when Congress placed the new capital, Washington, D.C., in the south, between Maryland and Virginia.

| George Washington, "father of our country"

Hamilton also wanted a national bank to store money raised by tariffs and a tax on whiskey. The Constitution did not say the government could make a bank. Jefferson argued the government could not do anything the Constitution did not specifically say. Hamilton argued that the Constitution allowed some things that were "necessary and proper" as part of collecting taxes. Washington agreed with Hamilton and signed the law creating the bank.

Political Parties. The first two political parties in America were the Federalists and the Democratic-Republicans. The Federalists were led by Alexander Hamilton, the Democratic-Republicans by Thomas Jefferson. The two parties opposed each other for president in 1796. Jefferson ran against John Adams, a Federalist. Adams won.

France was angry that America refused to help in its war in Europe. Adams sent men to discuss the problem. The French refused to talk unless they were paid a huge bribe. The Americans refused and went home. It was called the XYZ Affair, and the two countries almost went to war over it. However, the French eventually agreed to talk without a bribe. In 1800 the two sides agreed to end their alliance.

During the stir over the XYZ Affair, the Federalist Congress passed the Alien and Sedition Acts. These laws made it harder for

| John Adams

immigrants to become citizens. It also made it illegal to write bad things about the government. The law was used only to arrest Democratic-Republican writers. It made Adams very unpopular. When he ran against Jefferson again in 1800 for president, Jefferson won.

Answer these questions.

1.59 What was wrong with the Articles of Confederation?

_____

_____

1.60 What was the "Great Compromise" at the Constitutional Conventions?

_____

_____

1.61   What did the Northwest Ordinance do?

_____

_____

1.62   What are the three branches of the U.S. government?

_____

1.63   What was the name of the people who supported the Constitution?

a. _____

Those who opposed it? b. _____

1.64   What is the Bill of Rights?

_____

_____

1.65   Who was known as the "father of the Constitution"?

_____

1.66   Who was known as the "father of his country"?

_____

1.67   Who was the first president of the United States?

_____

1.68   What was the XYZ Affair?

_____

_____

1.69   What were the Alien and Sedition Acts?

_____

_____

1.70   What were the first two political parties in America, and who led them?

_____

_____

1.71   Who was the second president? a. _____

Who was the third president?   b. _____

1.72   Why was Washington, D.C. located in the south?

_____

_____

A Time of Testing

Louisiana Purchase. America grew substantially in 1803 when it purchased from France the land west of the Mississippi. France sold the land, named the Louisiana Purchase, for $15 million —about 3¢ an acre! It almost doubled the size of the country.

Jefferson sent out an expedition to explore and map the new land. The Lewis and Clark Expedition left in 1804. It went up the Missouri River, across the Rocky Mountains, down the Columbia River in Oregon to the Pacific Ocean and back. Along the way the men took careful notes and gathered samples.

Frontier. Hard life on the frontier made Americans strong and freedom loving. They were used to doing things for themselves and respected independent people. Frontier settlers, pioneers, kept moving west and founding more states that joined the Union. By 1820 America had 22 states. The frontier was a part of America up until about 1900.

Native Americans. The Indians of the Northwest Territory fought against the Americans as they tried to settle there. A Shawnee chief named Tecumseh organized an alliance of the Mississippi River tribes. The Tecumseh Confederacy was badly hurt when Tecumseh's brother was defeated by William Henry Harrison at the Battle of Tippecanoe in 1811. It fell apart in 1813 when Tecumseh was killed while fighting for the British in the War of 1812.

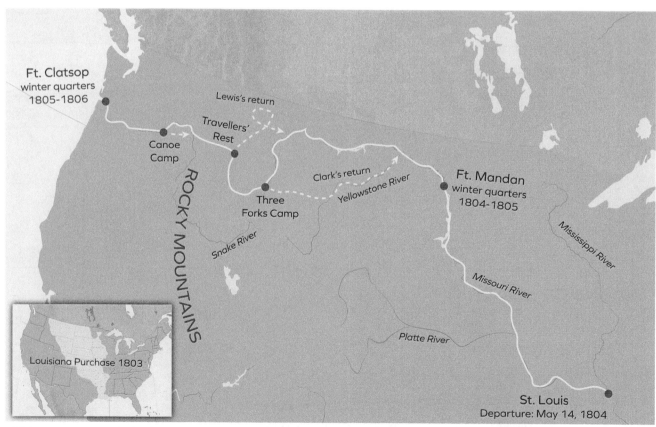

| The Lewis and Clark Expedition and the Louisiana Purchase

Embargo. War in Europe was causing some serious problems for America. Both Britain and France were stopping U.S. ships and taking cargoes that were going to the other side. Moreover, the British were impressing American sailors, "pressing" or forcing the men to serve in their navy. Jefferson was not willing to raise money for a navy to defend the ships.

Jefferson placed an embargo on all trade in 1807. By cutting off supplies to France and Britain, he hoped to avoid further seizures of American ships and their crews. All this embargo did was ruin U.S. trade and force thousands of people to lose their jobs. It was ended in 1809.

War Hawks. Around this time, many new congressmen were elected from the west and the south. These men were called the War Hawks because they wanted war with Britain. The new president, James Madison, tried other ideas, but all of them failed. In 1812 he asked Congress to declare war because of the taking of U.S. cargoes, impressment, British forts in U.S. territory, and the fact the British were giving guns to the Indians. The two-year war was called the War of 1812.

War of 1812. The U.S. began the war by invading Canada. The attacks failed and the British took Detroit. William Henry Harrison was put in command, and he ordered Oliver Perry to get the British off the Great Lakes. Perry built a fleet and defeated the British at the Battle of Lake Erie in 1813. Harrison caught the British when they left Detroit and defeated them at the Battle of the Thames River.

The British blockaded the American coast after several American victories in one-on-one ship battles. The British also landed an army that attacked and burned Washington, D.C. in 1814. They tried to attack Baltimore but were driven back. The failure of the British to take Fort McHenry in Baltimore Harbor inspired Francis Scott Key to write the "Star Spangled Banner," our national anthem.

| Andrew Jackson (a future president) led American troops in the War of 1812.

Treaty of Ghent. The British realized that only a long war would bring victory in America. They had been fighting in Europe for 20 years and were tired of war. Both sides met in Ghent in Europe and agreed to a treaty. The Treaty of Ghent ended the war and returned the land taken in battle. Nothing was said about impressment, but with the war over in Europe, it ended.

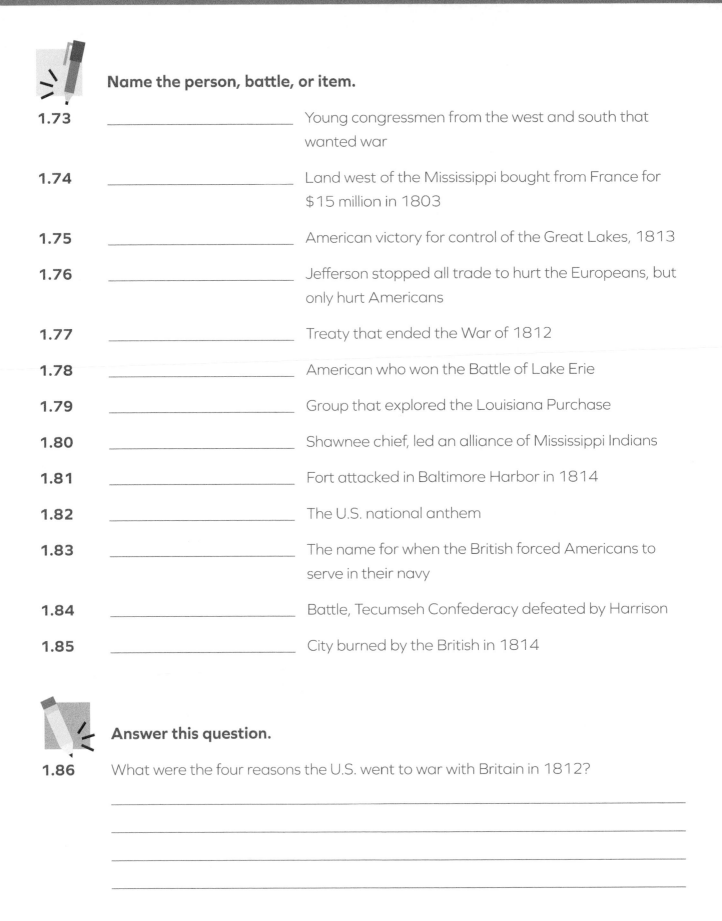

Name the person, battle, or item.

1.73 _____ Young congressmen from the west and south that wanted war

1.74 _____ Land west of the Mississippi bought from France for $15 million in 1803

1.75 _____ American victory for control of the Great Lakes, 1813

1.76 _____ Jefferson stopped all trade to hurt the Europeans, but only hurt Americans

1.77 _____ Treaty that ended the War of 1812

1.78 _____ American who won the Battle of Lake Erie

1.79 _____ Group that explored the Louisiana Purchase

1.80 _____ Shawnee chief, led an alliance of Mississippi Indians

1.81 _____ Fort attacked in Baltimore Harbor in 1814

1.82 _____ The U.S. national anthem

1.83 _____ The name for when the British forced Americans to serve in their navy

1.84 _____ Battle, Tecumseh Confederacy defeated by Harrison

1.85 _____ City burned by the British in 1814

Answer this question.

1.86 What were the four reasons the U.S. went to war with Britain in 1812?

_____

_____

_____

_____

New Orleans. The greatest American victory of the War of 1812 came after the treaty was signed. The British attacked the city of New Orleans in January of 1815, before news of the treaty reached America. Andrew Jackson defended the city. His men set up defensive walls and the British foolishly marched straight in to attack. Hundreds of British soldiers died, and less than twenty Americans were lost. The victory made Jackson a national hero.

There were two important results of the War of 1812. The first was nationalism or love of the nation. Americans believed they had won the war and were united as never before. The second result was that America began to be a manufacturing nation. The war stopped trade. Northern businessmen had built factories to supply the goods people needed. These men now wanted tariffs to raise the prices of foreign goods and protect their factories.

Florida. After the war, Indians and runaway slaves were raiding the U.S. from Florida. Andrew Jackson was sent in to stop the raids in 1819. Spain realized it could not hold the territory, so in the Adams-Onis Treaty, Spain gave the land to America. In turn, the U.S. government agreed to pay about $5 million worth of Spanish debts.

Missouri Compromise. In 1820 there were 11 slave states and 11 free states in the U.S. That year Missouri asked to be admitted as a slave state. The North did not want more slave states while the South did. Henry Clay found a compromise, called the Missouri Compromise. Missouri was admitted as a slave state and Maine as a free state. Also, slavery was forbidden north of Missouri's southern border (36° 30') in the Louisiana Purchase.

Monroe Doctrine. Many of the Spanish colonies had become independent during the wars in Europe. America was afraid that Europe would try to retake these colonies, so President James Monroe issued a statement called the Monroe Doctrine. It said that the countries of Europe could not take any colonies in the Americas that would threaten the United States. This doctrine would be an important part of U.S. foreign policy.

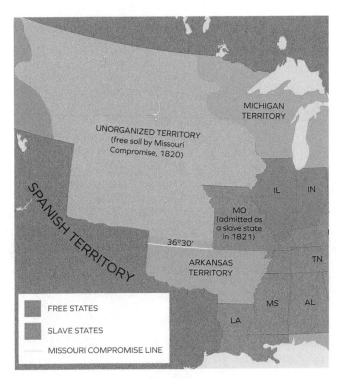

| Missouri Compromise

Sectionalism. After the Missouri Compromise, nationalism was replaced by sectionalism. People were more interested in the needs of their section of the country. The North wanted high tariffs, high land prices in the West, no federal money for roads or canals, and no slavery in the territories. The South wanted slavery in the territories, low tariffs, and no federal money for roads or canals. The West wanted low land prices and federal money for roads and canals. The North and South would argue over tariffs and slavery in the years leading up to the Civil War.

Political divide. In 1824 four men from the Democratic-Republican Party ran for president. Andrew Jackson got the most votes, but not enough. The House of Representatives had to decide the winner. Henry Clay, who had lost, convinced the House to vote for John Quincy Adams, who became president. Adams gave Henry Clay a job in his cabinet.

Jackson was furious. He believed the men had made a deal to take the presidency. The party split because of this. The Democrats followed Jackson. The Whigs followed Adams and Clay.

Roads. The federal government usually would not build roads, so businessmen began to build turnpikes—hard-surface toll roads. The first was the Lancaster Turnpike in Pennsylvania. One major federal road was the National or Cumberland Road that went from Cumberland, Maryland to Vandalia, Illinois. State roads connected it to Baltimore, Maryland on the Atlantic and to St. Louis, Missouri on the Mississippi River. St. Louis became the point where pioneers started their journey further west.

| Steamboats made moving cargo easier.

Steamboats. Rivers and lakes were better ways to ship large loads in the 1800s, but it was too much work to paddle a cargo boat up a river. In 1807 Robert Fulton invented the steamboat. His first ship, the *Clermont*, could travel upriver carrying a load of goods. These boats made two-way river trade possible, increasing trade and prosperity. They were especially important on the huge Mississippi River.

Canals. Canals were built to connect rivers and lakes for trade. These made shortcuts for shipping. The most successful canal was the Erie Canal in New York state. This canal connected the Great Lakes to the Mohawk and Hudson Rivers which flowed into the Atlantic Ocean. Built by the state of New York, it allowed western farmers around the Great Lakes to trade with the port cities of the East.

| The Erie Canal connected the Great Lakes to the Atlantic Ocean.

Give the information requested.

1.87 The inventor of the steamboat, his first ship, and the year it was invented:

_____

1.88 The greatest American victory of the War of 1812 and the commander:

_____

1.89 The two parties created when the Democratic-Republicans divided:

_____

1.90 Two important results of the War of 1812:

_____

1.91 What the Monroe Doctrine said:

_____

_____

1.92 The important federal road west from Baltimore to St. Louis:

_____

1.93 The most successful canal and what it connected:

_____

_____

1.94 Treaty that added Florida to the U.S. and the soldier who pushed Spain to sign it:

_____

1.95 Terms of the Missouri Compromise:

_____

_____

_____

1.96   When sectionalism occurred, what the North wanted:

a. _____

_____

What the South wanted:

b. _____

_____

What the West wanted:

c. _____

_____

Review the material in this section to prepare for the Self Test. The Self Test will check your understanding of this section. Any items you miss on this test will show you what areas you will need to restudy in order to prepare for the unit test.

SELF TEST 1

Match these people (each answer, 2 points).

1.01 _____ Led the first Europeans to reach America

1.02 _____ Invented the cotton gin, used interchangeable parts to make guns

1.03 _____ Set up the Missouri Compromise

1.04 _____ Explored and named Florida

1.05 _____ Led the founding of Georgia for debtors

1.06 _____ "Father of New France," founded Quebec

1.07 _____ Discovered America while trying to reach Asia for Spain

1.08 _____ Revolutionary War commander, first president

1.09 _____ Revolutionary War hero, traitor

1.010 _____ Explored a river in New York for the Dutch and a bay in Canada for the English

1.011 _____ Hero of the Battle of New Orleans, also forced Spain to give up Florida to the U.S.

1.012 _____ Wealthy Quaker, founder of Delaware and Pennsylvania

1.013 _____ Second president

1.014 _____ Third president, wrote the Declaration of Independence

1.015 _____ Founded Rhode Island

a. Christopher Columbus

b. Ponce de Leon

c. Samuel de Champlain

d. Henry Hudson

e. George Washington

f. William Penn

g. Roger Williams

h. Thomas Jefferson

i. Benedict Arnold

j. Eli Whitney

k. John Adams

l. Henry Clay

m. Andrew Jackson

n. Leif Ericson

o. James Oglethorpe

Name the item, war, event, or thing (each answer, 3 points).

1.016 _____ New France was around the Great Lakes, the St. Lawrence River, and this river

1.017 _____ New Netherlands became this colony (later a state) when it was taken over by England

1.018 _____ The first English colony in America

1.019 _____ War between England and France (1754-1763), France lost its American lands

1.020 _____ First battle of the American Revolutionary War

1.021 _____ Last important battle of the Revolutionary War

1.022 _____ Boston's reaction to taxed tea in 1773

1.023 _____ War against Britain over impressment, the capture of U.S. cargoes, and British forts on American land

1.024 _____ Land west of the Mississippi River purchased from France in 1803 for 3¢ an acre

1.025 _____ First ten amendments to the Constitution

Match these items (each answer, 2 points).

1.026	_____ America's first Constitution, did not give Congress the power to tax	a. Portugal
		b. Northwest Passage
1.027	_____ Brought the Separatists to Plymouth	c. fur
1.028	_____ Closed Boston Harbor, took away freedoms in Massachusetts	d. *Mayflower*
		e. *Clermont*
1.029	_____ Taxes on lead, paint, and tea	f. Maryland
1.030	_____ First steamboat, built by Robert Fulton	g. Townshend Acts
		h. Articles of Confederation
1.031	_____ National anthem, written about the defense of Fort McHenry in Baltimore, War of 1812	i. Intolerable Act
		j. Saratoga
		k. Federalist
1.032	_____ French wanted this product from the New World	l. Great Compromise
		m. XYZ Affair
1.033	_____ Constitutional Convention, it was agreed that all states would get the same vote in the Senate and would get votes by population in the House	n. Lewis and Clark
		o. Star Spangled Banner

1.034 _____ A British Army was captured by the Americans, France became a U.S. ally in the Revolution

1.035 _____ Colony set up as a refuge for Catholics by Lord Baltimore

1.036 _____ Many men who explored the New World were looking for this, a way through America to Asia

1.037 _____ The French refused to negotiate with President John Adams' representatives unless a huge bribe was paid first

1.038 _____ First nation to find an all-water route from Europe to Asia

1.039 _____ Explored the Louisiana Purchase

1.040 _____ Political party that favored the U.S. Constitution

Answer *true* or *false* (each answer, 1 point).

1.041 _____ The first people to reach America were the Native Americans (Indians).

1.042 _____ Hernando de Soto was a fur trader who explored the St. Lawrence River and discovered the Grand Banks.

1.043 _____ North Carolina was settled by Puritans fleeing persecution in England. They built large cotton plantations there.

1.044 _____ The American colonists had to retreat at the Battle of Bunker Hill after they ran out of gunpowder.

1.045 _____ The British had all the advantages in the Revolutionary War.

1.046 _____ Baron von Steuben led a British attack on the American Army at Valley Forge in the Revolutionary War.

1.047 _____ Nathanael Greene drove the British out of the south in the Revolutionary War by winning several large, important battles.

1.048 _____ The triangle trade brought slaves across the Middle Passage to the West Indies from Africa to trade them for molasses for America.

1.049 _____ James Madison opposed the Constitution and almost succeeded in preventing it from being ratified.

1.050 _____ The first two political parties to contest an election in America were the Whigs and the Republicans in 1796.

Teacher check:
Score _____
Initials _____
Date _____
80/100

2. STRONGER AMERICA (1830 - 1930)

This section will review the events that happened when our nation was growing from about 1830 to 1920. During this time, the United States spread across the continent. It was then divided by the Civil War, went through a time of corruption and reform, won an easy war with a European power, and joined in a world-wide war in Europe. America grew in these years from a backward farming nation into one of the most powerful manufacturing nations on earth. This section will take you back through these years again.

Objective

Review the objective. When you have completed this section, you should be able to:

■ Give a general overview of American history, recognizing important people, inventions, wars, and events.

A Growing Nation

Jackson. Andrew Jackson was elected president in 1828. He was the first U.S. president who was not born into a wealthy family. He was born poor, earned his own fortune, and lived in the west (Tennessee). He was wildly popular and had strong ideas about being president. He vetoed more laws than all six of the presidents before him. The ordinary man began to be important in American politics after Andrew Jackson.

Jackson encouraged the "spoils system" which gave government jobs to his supporters. He vetoed a charter for the National Bank, which he did not trust, and took federal money out of it. The money was put in state banks ("pet banks"), and the National Bank was closed. Jackson also threatened to use force when South Carolina nullified the tariff in 1832 by refusing to allow it to be collected in their state. Henry Clay ("the Great Compromiser") arranged for the tariff to be lowered, and Carolina backed down. Jackson also moved thousands of Native Americans from their land east of the Mississippi to Oklahoma so that American pioneers could have their land. Many died on the journey, later known as the "Trail of Tears."

After Jackson. Andrew Jackson chose his vice president, Martin Van Buren, to run for the presidency when he retired. With Jackson's support, Van Buren won the election in 1836. However, a depression in 1837 (also called a "panic") made him very unpopular.

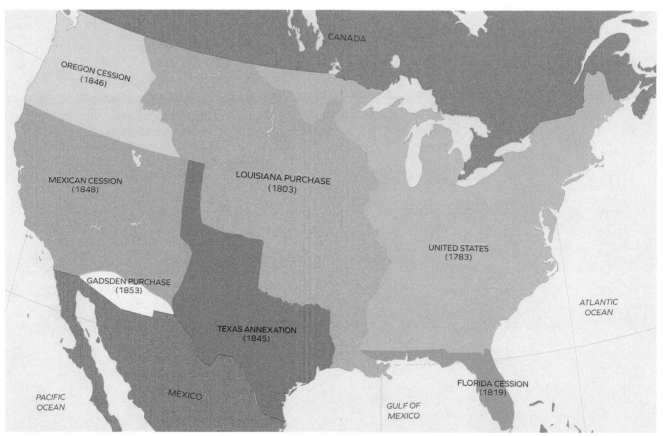

| Major acquisitions of the United States

The Whig Party ran the military hero William Henry Harrison for president in 1840. Harrison had won the Battle of Tippecanoe, so the Whigs used the slogan "Tippecanoe and Tyler, too!" John Tyler was Harrison's running mate. Harrison was pictured as the "Log Cabin and Hard Cider" candidate, a man of the people (like Jackson). He won, but only lived a month after being elected.

John Tyler, the new Whig president, vetoed many of the laws passed by the Whigs in Congress. They began to hate him and did not support him for re-election in 1844. The Democratic candidate, James Polk, campaigned for Manifest Destiny, the idea that it was the obvious (manifest) future (destiny) of the U.S. to spread across the continent. Polk won and added more land to America than any other president.

Lone Star Republic. Many Americans moved to Texas in the early 1800s, with the permission of Spain and Mexico. These settlers revolted in 1834 when a dictator named Santa Anna took over the Mexican government. The Texans declared their independence in 1836, creating a republic.

War for Texas independence. Santa Anna brought a huge Mexican Army into Texas to crush the revolt. In 1836 he killed all of the men defending a mission in San Antonio called the Alamo. Sam Houston, the commander of the Texas army, defeated Santa Anna at the Battle of San Jacinto a month later. Santa Anna was captured and signed a treaty giving Texas its independence.

| Frontiersman Davy Crockett fought and died at the Alamo.

Sam Houston was elected as the republic's first president, and it asked to join the Union. However, Mexico threatened to go to war if Texas joined the U.S., and the northern states did not want such a large slave state, so Texas remained a republic until 1845. In 1844 James Polk campaigned for annexing Texas. When Polk won, Texas was annexed.

Oregon. Oregon was held by both the U.S. and Britain under the terms of an 1818 treaty. However, in the 1840s thousands of American settlers poured into the region on the Oregon Trail, a difficult 2,000 mile, six-month journey across the Great Plains and the Rocky Mountains. Many Americans wanted all of Oregon, up to 54° 40' (now the southern edge of Alaska) even if it meant war with Britain. These people made up the famous slogan, "Fifty-four Forty or Fight." Polk, however, was willing to compromise. In 1846 he agreed to divide Oregon by extending the U.S./Canadian border at 49° latitude.

Mexican War. Having added Texas and Oregon to the United States, Polk next tried to get California; however, Mexico would not sell it. Therefore, Polk sent American troops under the command of Zachary Taylor south of the Nueces River in Texas. The Mexicans claimed that the Nueces River, not the Rio Grande, was the border. The Mexican Army attacked the Americans on "their" land, and Polk had Congress declare war.

| The Americans defeated the Mexican Army at the Battle of Chapultepec.

Taylor captured the Mexican cities of Matamoros and Monterrey in 1846. He then defeated a Mexican Army three times the size of his at the Battle of Buena Vista in 1847. The victories made him a hero, and he was later elected president (1849).

General Winfield Scott captured Mexico City in 1847 and ended the war. In the Treaty of Guadalupe Hidalgo, Mexico sold to the U.S. all of the land between, and including, Texas and California, as well as parts of present-day Colorado, Nevada, and Utah. The U.S. paid $15 million for the Mexican Cession, which at that time was the largest piece of land added to the Union since the Louisiana Purchase.

The last piece of land added to the continental U.S. was bought from Mexico in 1853. The U.S. needed the land for a railroad route across the south to California. The Gadsden Purchase cost America $10 million.

Inventions. Several inventions in the 1830s and 1840s helped the nation to grow. The steel plow, invented by John Deere, and the mechanical reaper, invented by Cyrus McCormick, allowed farmers to work more land with fewer people. The telegraph, invented by Samuel Morse, allowed messages to be sent instantly anywhere in the country. Most important, the railroad connected the cities of America.

Compromise of 1850. Gold was discovered in California in 1848 at Sutter's Mill. Because of a gold rush, there were enough people there to apply for statehood in 1850; however, the South did not want another free state. Henry Clay arranged the Compromise of 1850. California was admitted as a free state and the South was given a Fugitive Slave Act.

The Fugitive Slave Act was to catch slaves that were escaping to freedom in the North on the Underground Railroad, an organization which helped guide and protect escaping slaves on their journey north. The Fugitive Slave Act fined and imprisoned people who helped escaped slaves. It also made it easier to take slaves back to their masters when they were caught. The North hated the law and interfered with it.

Abolition. Many reforms came after the Second Great Awakening, a revival in the early 1800s. The most important was the abolitionist movement to end slavery. The most famous abolitionist book was *Uncle Tom's Cabin* by Harriet Beecher Stowe, published in 1852. It showed slaves to be real people who were truly suffering. Many people in the North turned against slavery because of it.

Kansas-Nebraska Act. In 1854 the Kansas-Nebraska Act allowed the settlers in those territories to decide the issue of slavery themselves. However, both those territories were north of the Missouri Compromise line and should not have allowed slavery. The North was furious at the change. Kansas became known as "Bleeding Kansas" because of constant fighting between the settlers who wanted slavery and those who did not.

Dred Scott Decision. The Supreme Court made matters worse in 1857 with the Dred Scott case. Scott was a slave who lived in the North and sued for his freedom. The five southern justices outvoted the four northern ones and said that slaves were property protected by the Constitution. That meant slavery was legal in all of the United States. The North refused to accept this.

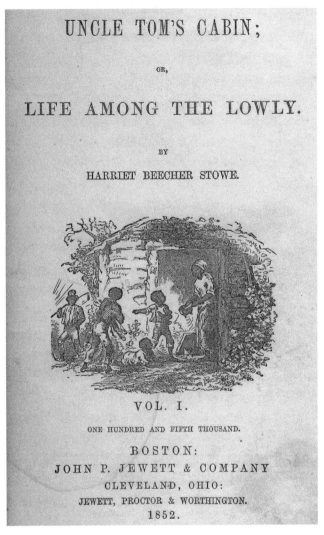

| *Uncle Tom's Cabin* turned many against slavery.

Lincoln-Douglas Debates. A series of famous debates was held in 1858 in Illinois by two men running for the U.S. Senate. Stephen Douglas argued that people should be able to choose for themselves whether or not to oppose slavery. His opponent, Abraham Lincoln, was from the new anti-slavery Republican Party. Lincoln said that slavery was morally wrong and should not be allowed to spread into the new territories. Lincoln lost the election but gained national attention for his stand.

John Brown's Raid. A violent abolitionist named John Brown tried to start a slave rebellion in 1859. He attacked the U.S. arsenal at Harpers Ferry, Virginia to get weapons. He was caught and hung. Many northerners thought he was a hero, and he became a martyr to the abolitionists.

Election of 1860. When Abraham Lincoln was elected president in 1860, the South decided that was enough. They no longer trusted the North. They expected more attacks like John Brown's raid, and now the U.S. had a president who openly opposed slavery.

Right after the election, South Carolina, followed by six other southern states, seceded from the Union. They formed their own country called the Confederate States of America with Jefferson Davis as president. The U.S. president, James Buchanan (who was in office until Lincoln was inaugurated in March of 1861), did not try to stop them.

Name the president.

2.1 _____ Spoils System

2.2 _____ Tippecanoe and Tyler, too

2.3 _____ Nullification Crisis

2.4 _____ Panic of 1837

2.5 _____ Became president when Harrison died

2.6 _____ Added more land to the Union than any other

2.7 _____ First president born poor

2.8 _____ Log Cabin and Hard Cider

2.9 _____ Campaigned for Manifest Destiny

2.10 _____ Trail of Tears

2.11 _____ Shut down the National Bank

2.12 _____ Vetoed his own party's laws

2.13 _____ Mexican War

2.14 _____ Oregon and Mexican Cessions

2.15 _____ Did not try to stop the southern states from seceding

2.16 _____ Openly said slavery was wrong

2.17 _____ Mexican War hero

HISTORY & GEOGRAPHY 510

LIFEPAC TEST

85

106

NAME _____

DATE _____

SCORE _____

Name the war or major event based on the battles, events, and people (each answer, 2 points).

1. _____ The *Maine* blew up, America accepted as a world power, Rough Riders (1898)

2. _____ The national anthem, Battle of Lake Erie, fought with Britain over impressment (1812-1814)

3. _____ Midway, Stalingrad, D-day, Island Hopping (1939-1945)

4. _____ Lexington and Concord, Saratoga, Yorktown, American independence (1776-1783)

5. _____ Unrestricted submarine warfare, Archduke Ferdinand assassinated (1914–1918)

6. _____ Stock Market Crash of 1929, New Deal, 1 in 4 out of work

7. _____ Longest, most controversial war in U.S. history, Gulf of Tonkin Resolution, 1960s and 1970s

8. _____ Mexican Cession, Zachary Taylor, Buena Vista, Winfield Scott

9. _____ Fort Sumter, Gettysburg, Appomattox Courthouse, Robert E. Lee (1861-1865)

10. _____ Between France and Britain in America, France lost all its colonies (1754-1763)

Match these people (each answer, 2 points).

11. _____ Found America trying to reach Asia for Spain

12. _____ New Deal, elected to 4 terms, World War II

13. _____ Commander, Revolutionary War; 1st president

14. _____ Wrote the Declaration of Independence

15. _____ Added more land to the U.S. than any other president

16. _____ Only president to resign from office

17. _____ Civil War, Emancipation Proclamation

18. _____ Founded Delaware & Pennsylvania colonies

19. _____ President, World War II army general

20. _____ First president born poor, vetoed the National Bank, threatened S. Carolina in Nullification Crisis

a. George Washington
b. William Penn
c. Thomas Jefferson
d. Abraham Lincoln
e. Franklin D. Roosevelt
f. Dwight Eisenhower
g. Andrew Jackson
h. Richard Nixon
i. James Polk
j. Christopher Columbus

Match these items (each answer, 2 points).

21. _____ Expedition that explored the Louisiana Purchase

22. _____ Line between communist and free Europe

23. _____ Conflict of ideas, alliances and fear between the U.S. and U.S.S.R. from 1945 to 1989

24. _____ City hit by an atomic bomb, World War II

25. _____ Organization that helped slaves escape north

26. _____ Reforms, began in the cities, 1890s to 1917

27. _____ Political party that wanted the Constitution to be ratified after it was written

28. _____ Gave land to citizens who lived on it 5 years

29. _____ Time of abuse of power and corruption after the Civil War

30. _____ Land bought from Mexico to allow a railroad route along the southern U.S.

31. _____ First 10 Amendments to the Constitution

32. _____ Indians were forced to move to Oklahoma

33. _____ Woodrow Wilson's plan for peace, World War I

34. _____ Time of rebuilding the South after the Civil War

35. _____ Forbade slavery north of the southern border of Missouri

36. _____ British laws that closed Boston Harbor after the Boston Tea Party

37. _____ Japanese attack, brought the U.S. into World War II

38. _____ Scandal when the cover-up after a burglary forced the president to resign

39. _____ Forbade the sale of alcohol in the U.S.

40. _____ The murder of millions of people, especially Jews, by the Nazis in World War II

a. Homestead Act
b. Intolerable Acts
c. Reconstruction
d. Missouri Compromise
e. Cold War
f. Watergate
g. Lewis and Clark
h. Fourteen Points
i. Bill of Rights
j. Prohibition
k. Holocaust
l. Pearl Harbor
m. Progressive
n. Iron Curtain
o. Gadsden Purchase
p. Gilded Age
q. Federalist
r. Underground Railroad
s. Trail of Tears
t. Hiroshima

Answer *true* or *false* (each answer, 2 points).

41. _____ Virginia, Missouri, and Texas were part of the original thirteen colonies.

42. _____ Eli Whitney, Thomas Edison, and Alexander Bell were U.S. presidents.

43. _____ Norman Schwarzkopf, Douglas MacArthur, and Benedict Arnold were American generals.

44. _____ The Marshall Plan gave money to Europe to rebuild after World War II.

45. _____ The Abolitionist Movement failed in the United States.

46. _____ Martin Luther King, Henry Clay, and Boris Yeltsin were inventors.

47. _____ No U.S. presidents have ever been impeached.

48. _____ The Civil War gave black slaves their freedom, but they were not given legal equality until the Civil Rights Movement.

49. _____ The three parts of the U.S. government, under the Constitution, are the legislative, military, and presidential.

50. _____ Manifest Destiny was the idea that it was America's obvious future to defeat Communism.

51. _____ Saddam Hussein planned the September 11, 2001, terrorist attacks against the United States.

52. _____ Osama bin Laden headed the Al Qaeda organization in Afghanistan.

53. _____ Barack Obama became the first African-American president of the United States in 2000.

Match these items. Some will be used more than once.

2.18	_____ Mexico City captured by Winfield Scott	a. Texas Republic
2.19	_____ Supreme Court—slavery was legal in all America	b. Oregon
2.20	_____ Harpers Ferry, Virginia	c. Mexican War
2.21	_____ Seven states seceded from the Union at this	d. Alamo
2.22	_____ Henry Clay	e. Abolition
2.23	_____ Lincoln became known throughout the nation	f. Telegraph
2.24	_____ Samuel Morse invented it	g. Compromise of 1850
2.25	_____ California admitted as a free state	h. Kansas-Nebraska Act
2.26	_____ Caused Bleeding Kansas	i. Dred Scott Decision
2.27	_____ Broke the Missouri Compromise	j. Lincoln-Douglas Debates
2.28	_____ Thousands of settlers came on the 2,000-mile trail, traveling for six months	k. John Brown's raid
2.29	_____ Reform movement to end slavery	l. Lincoln's election as president
2.30	_____ Fugitive Slave Act passed	m. Underground Railroad
2.31	_____ U.S. paid $15 million	
2.32	_____ All the defenders were killed	
2.33	_____ People who helped slaves escape to freedom	
2.34	_____ Won its independence at San Jacinto	
2.35	_____ U.S. got the Mexican Cession	
2.36	_____ This reform group's most famous book was *Uncle Tom's Cabin*	
2.37	_____ Lincoln said slavery was wrong and should not spread	
2.38	_____ Tried to start a slave rebellion, abolitionist martyr	
2.39	_____ Lasted for 9 years after independence from Mexico	
2.40	_____ Shared by U.S. and Britain before 1846	

A Nation Divided

The Civil War. The Civil War began in 1861 and ended in 1865. It began in April of 1861 when Confederate soldiers (from the seven states that had seceded) fired on Union soldiers at Fort Sumter in Charleston Harbor (South Carolina). Four more states seceded after that, bringing the number of Confederate states to eleven.

The Union had the advantage in men, factories, railroads, and a navy (which they used to blockade southern ports). However, the Confederacy still won most of the early battles in the east because they had better generals, particularly their commander, Robert E. Lee.

The Union, however, did win the early battles in the west. Union general Ulysses S. Grant captured the last major Confederate stronghold on the Mississippi River at Vicksburg in May of 1863. That same year the Union won the Battle of Gettysburg in Pennsylvania, which was the turning point of the war. The Confederacy usually lost the battles after that. Also, the Union blockade had cut off supplies of food, clothing, and weapons for the South.

The North originally fought to save the Union. However, in September of 1861, President Lincoln issued the Emancipation Proclamation which declared that all of the slaves in the South were free. The Thirteenth Amendment to the Constitution later ended slavery for the whole nation.

After his victories in the west, Grant was put in command of the entire Union Army in 1864. He pursued and attacked Lee until the Confederates were forced to surrender in April of 1865 at Appomattox Courthouse, Virginia. Lee's surrender was the end of the war. The Union was restored and slavery was finally ended.

Reconstruction. President Lincoln was assassinated just days after Lee surrendered. The new president, Andrew Johnson, wanted to make it easy for the southern states to rejoin the Union. He used Lincoln's plan, called the Ten Percent Plan, that allowed them to rejoin when just ten percent of the men had sworn loyalty to the United States. The southern states quickly did this. However, they also passed Black Codes that were just like slavery for the freedmen and sent former Confederate leaders as representatives to Congress. That angered the northern congressmen.

A group in Congress called the Radical Republicans took control of Reconstruction. This was called Radical Reconstruction. Congress passed the 14th Amendment which made the freed slaves citizens and demanded that the southern states approve it. The states that did not were divided into five military districts under the control of a Union general. Congress also passed the 15th Amendment, which gave black men the right to vote. Congress became so frustrated with President Johnson that they impeached him in 1868. The Radicals lost in the Senate trial, however. Johnson won by one vote and stayed on as president.

The troops in the South forced the states to register black voters who elected Reconstruction governments that were often Republican. Southern whites hated these governments, calling the northerners in them "Carpetbaggers" and the southerners "Scalawags." Southerners eventually used violence to stop the blacks from voting. In this way, they regained control of their state governments.

Because of hatred over Reconstruction, the South voted only Democratic for years. Blacks were kept separate and oppressed in the South for almost a hundred years. Reconstruction officially ended in 1877 when newly-elected President Rutherford B. Hayes agreed to end it. In exchange, the Democratic Party accepted that Hayes had won the 1876 election, even though it looked like the Democratic candidate had won.

Gilded Age. The time after the Civil War was called the Gilded Age. It was a time of large corporations that made many men very wealthy. The railroads were the first of these large corporations. In 1869 they completed the first transcontinental railroad, opening the west to settlers.

| During the Gilded Age, wealthy industrialists built lavish mansions

The Homestead Act gave 160 acres of land to anyone who would live on it for five years. With the help of the railroads, thousands of settlers flocked to the Great Plains to homestead. They blocked off the long trails from Texas that the cowboys had used from 1870 to 1890 to drive cattle to railroad towns. By about 1890, there was no longer a frontier in America except for the new territory of Alaska, purchased from Russia in 1867.

The many new corporations made men rich, creating a "High Society" in which money was spent lavishly. Among the new rich, Andrew Carnegie made his fortune in steel, using the new, cheaper Bessemer Process. John D. Rockefeller made his fortune controlling oil production in America with his company, Standard Oil. Inventors like Alexander Bell (the telephone) and Thomas Edison (the phonograph and the electric light bulb) gave business new products to build and sell.

This rapid growth of industry and wealth created widespread corruption and abuse of power. Poor immigrants and city dwellers worked for low pay and lived in poverty while working in the new factories. The industrialists gave money to support congressmen to keep the tariff high. This meant they could charge more for their products. That hurt farmers who had to buy manufactured goods at protected prices but sold their crops without any tariff protection. The farmers were also charged unfairly by the railroads to ship their crops. The industrialists also formed trusts which controlled all the sales of one product in the country.

The public demanded reforms, especially of the Civil Service or government jobs. These jobs went to supporters of the party in power, and the workers had to pay the party some of their salary to keep their positions. Finally, Congress passed the Pendleton Act that gave the jobs to people who did the best on a special test. It took years to put most government jobs under this system. Other reform laws were also passed. The Sherman Anti-Trust Act was passed to break up trusts that were cheating the public. The Interstate Commerce Act was passed to control the railroads. However, none of these were enforced during the Gilded Age, a time when abuse of power and corruption ruled.

| Factory workers often worked long hours in dangerous conditions.

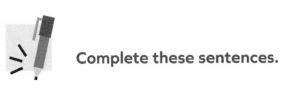

Complete these sentences.

2.41   At the end of the Civil War, the Union commander was General _____

and the Confederate commander was General _____ .

2.42   During the Civil War, the _____ had the advantage in men,

factories, and railroads. Yet, the _____ won most of the early

battles in the east because of better generals.

2.43   The Civil War began at _____ , it turned in favor of the

North at _____ and ended at _____ .

2.44   The president of the U.S. during the Civil War was _____ .

The president of the Confederacy was _____ .

2.45   Slavery was ended in the South by the _____ of

1861. The _____ Amendment ended it in the rest of the country.

2.46   After Lincoln's assassination, the new president, _____ ,

tried an easy Reconstruction plan called the _____ Plan.

2.47   The leaders of a harsh Reconstruction plan were the _____ .

2.48   The _____ Amendment made black people citizens and the

_____ Amendment gave black men the right to vote.

2.49   In the hated Reconstruction governments, northerners were called

_____ and southerners _____ .

2.50   The southern whites used _____ to regain control and

voted only for the _____ Party for many years.

2.51   Reconstruction was ended in _____ by President _____ .

2.52   The time after the Civil War was called the _____ Age.

2.53   The _____ Act gave 160 acres to anyone who lived

on the land for five years.

2.54   The first transcontinental railroad was finished in _____ .

2.55   Andrew Carnegie made his fortune in _____ while

John D. Rockefeller made his in _____ .

2.56   The telephone was invented by _____ while the

            electric light bulb and phonograph were invented by _____ .

2.57   The _____ Act was to reform the Civil Service, and the

            Interstate Commerce Act was to control the _____ .

2.58   Two things that hurt farmers were the _____ and the

            _____ .

2.59   A _____ controlled all sales of one product.

2.60   The Gilded Age was a time of _____ and abuse of power.

A Changing Nation

The Progressive Era. Beginning in the 1890s and lasting until about 1917, America went though a time of reform called the Progressive Era. The reformers began in the cities. They ended the control of party bosses and forced city governments to provide good services, like water and electricity, for the citizens. They passed laws making city apartments safer and cleaner. In the states, the reformers controlled the railroads, started primary elections (elections by a political party to choose a candidate), and passed fair taxes. New laws and work by unions made wages higher, stopped child labor, and improved working conditions in factories.

We had three Progressive presidents: Theodore Roosevelt, William H. Taft, and Woodrow Wilson. Roosevelt was the first president to use the Sherman Anti-Trust Act to break up trusts. He also improved controls on the railroads, was fair to coal miners who went on strike, and created many national parks. Roosevelt also used his "Big Stick" ideas on foreign policy to help Panama rebel against Columbia so the U.S. could get land for the Panama Canal. Taft continued the anti-trust work and tried to reduce the tariff. Wilson did reduce the tariff and set up the Federal Reserve system to control the banks. World War I stopped the reforms, and they did not continue after the war was finished.

THE BIG STICK IN THE CARIBBEAN SEA

| 1904 cartoon of Roosevelt and his 'Big Stick' ideology.

Spanish-American War. Cuba rebelled against Spain in the mid-1890s. Americans favored Cuban independence, and the "yellow press" wrote stories about how cruel the Spanish were. In February of 1898, the U.S. Battleship *Maine* blew up in Havana Harbor. Americans blamed Spain, and the U.S. declared war. George Dewey destroyed the Spanish fleet in the Philippines. A U.S. Army that included Theodore Roosevelt's Rough Riders attacked Santiago. They captured the city, and the Spanish fleet was destroyed. The U.S. won the war in a few months, taking Guam, the Philippines, and Puerto Rico as colonies. The war marked the point at which America was recognized as a world power.

World War I. In 1914 the nations of Europe were having an arms race and were divided into two alliances. The Allies included Britain, France, and Russia. The Central Powers included Germany, Austria-Hungary, and Italy (which later joined the Allies). War broke out in 1914 after the heir to the throne of Austria-Hungary, Archduke Ferdinand, was assassinated in Sarajevo, Bosnia. Germany invaded France through neutral Belgium. The two sides fought to a standstill in the west, building a long line of trenches that ran from the sea to Switzerland.

The U.S. was isolationist and wanted to stay out of the war. However, Germany began sinking ships going to Britain and France using U-boats (submarines). When they announced unrestricted submarine warfare, the U.S. declared war in 1917. It took America a year to get a large army to Europe. The American Expeditionary Force under General John Pershing, however, turned the war in favor of the Allies in 1918. Germany signed an armistice in November of 1918.

| General John "Black Jack" Pershing

The peace treaty was negotiated at the Paris Peace Conference. Woodrow Wilson had his own plan for a fair peace called the Fourteen Points, but most of the Allies did not want a fair peace. Germany was forced to take full responsibility for the war and pay its costs. This made Germany very poor, and eventually they became willing to accept a dictator, Adolf Hitler, who started the next war in 1939. The Conference did create an association of nations called the League of Nations that Wilson had asked for in his Fourteen Points; however, the U.S. never joined it.

The Roaring Twenties. After the war, America wanted to stay out of world problems and just enjoy life. Americans spent money on things like automobiles, radios, movies, baseball games, and parties. Women called "flappers" wore shorter skirts, make-up, and smoked in public.

Much of the spending of the 1920s was done using credit (borrowing). Businesses prospered because people were spending money to buy their goods. The Republican presidents of the 1920s favored business. They increased the tariff and did not push reforms. This was a time of fun and spending called the Roaring Twenties.

It was illegal to sell alcohol in the 1920s. This was called Prohibition. However, people drank anyway. They went to illegal bars called speakeasies. Criminals got rich making and selling alcohol. Prohibition was finally ended in 1933.

In the 1920s, the buying and spending made the businesses rich. This made prices go up on the stock market because the businesses were more valuable. Many people began to speculate in the stock market, borrowing money to buy stock, then selling it when the price went up. However, in October of 1929, the stock market crashed. People lost billions of dollars as the prices fell lower and lower. This started the Great Depression.

Answer these questions.

2.61 What started World War I?_____

_____

2.62 What started the Spanish-American War? _____

_____

2.63 What was the name of the time of reforms around the beginning of the 20th century?

_____

2.64 Why did America get into World War I? _____

2.65 Who were the three Progressive presidents?_____

_____

2.66 What was the name of the wild time of spending in the 1920s?

_____

2.67 What was the time in the 1920s when alcohol was illegal in the U.S. called?

_____

2.68 What was the name of the association of nations after World War I?

_____

2.69 What event marked the point that America was recognized as a world power?

_____

2.70 What started the Great Depression?

_____

_____

2.71 What was the name of Woodrow Wilson's peace plan?

_____

2.72 What was used for much of the spending of the 1920s?

_____

2.73 Who was the commander of the American Expeditionary Force?

_____

2.74 What nation was forced to take responsibility for World War I and pay its costs?

_____

Review the material in this section to prepare for the Self Test. The Self Test will check your understanding of this section and the previous section. Any items you miss on this test will show you what areas you will need to restudy in order to prepare for the unit test.

SELF TEST 2

Match these people (each answer, 2 points).

2.01	_____ President, impeached by Radical Republicans	a. Andrew Jackson
2.02	_____ Made his fortune with Standard Oil	b. Abraham Lincoln
2.03	_____ Rough Rider, used "Big Stick" to get Panama Canal	c. Sam Houston
2.04	_____ Invented the light bulb and phonograph	d. William Henry Harrison
		e. Andrew Johnson
2.05	_____ President, added more land to the U.S. than any other president	f. James Polk
		g. Samuel Morse
2.06	_____ Invented the telegraph	h. Alexander Bell
2.07	_____ President one month, "Tippecanoe and Tyler, too"	i. Andrew Carnegie
		j. Thomas Edison
2.08	_____ Progressive president, World War I	k. Ulysses S. Grant
2.09	_____ Civil War president, assassinated	l. Robert E. Lee
2.010	_____ Union general, Civil War	m. John D. Rockefeller
2.011	_____ Invented the telephone	n. Woodrow Wilson
2.012	_____ President of the Republic of Texas	o. Theodore Roosevelt
2.013	_____ Confederate general	
2.014	_____ President, spoils system, Nullification Crisis, first one born poor	
2.015	_____ Made his fortune in steel with the Bessemer Process	

Name the war or conflict (each answer, 3 points).

2.016 _____ The *Maine* blew up, the Philippines were captured, America was recognized as a world power

2.017 _____ Archduke Ferdinand's assassination started it, unrestricted submarine warfare got America involved

2.018 _____ The Alamo, San Jacinto, Sam Houston's army fought against Santa Anna

2.019 _____ Buena Vista, Zachary Taylor, and Winfield Scott were heroes, resulted in the Mexican Cession

2.020 _____ Fort Sumter, Gettysburg, and Appomattox Courthouse

Match these items (each answer, 2 points).

2.021 _____ Time of corruption and abuse of power after the Civil War

2.022 _____ Reform movement to end slavery

2.023 _____ Woodrow Wilson's peace plan, World War I

2.024 _____ Time of fun and free spending after World War I

2.025 _____ Indians were forced to move to Oklahoma

2.026 _____ Gave land to any citizen who would live on it for five years

2.027 _____ Made drinking alcohol illegal

2.028 _____ Organization to help slaves escape to the North

2.029 _____ Law to break up damaging trusts

2.030 _____ Lincoln declared all the slaves in the South were free

2.031 _____ California was admitted as a free state, the Fugitive Slave Act was passed

2.032 _____ The Supreme Court said slavery was legal and protected in all of the U.S.

2.033 _____ Reform movement at the end of the 1800s, began in the cities

2.034 _____ The rebuilding of the South after the Civil War

2.035 _____ Route used by thousands to cross the Great Plains and Rocky Mountains, a six-month journey

a. Trail of Tears

b. Compromise of 1850

c. Oregon Trail

d. Emancipation Proclamation

e. Underground Railroad

f. Dred Scott Decision

g. Fourteen Points

h. Gilded Age

i. Reconstruction

j. Sherman Anti-Trust

k. Homestead Act

l. Progressive

m. Roaring Twenties

n. Prohibition

o. Abolition

Answer these questions (each answer, 3 points).

2.036 What was Manifest Destiny?

_____

_____

_____

2.037 What did the Thirteenth Amendment do?

_____

_____

_____

2.038 Why was _Uncle Tom's Cabin_ such an important book?

_____

_____

_____

2.039 What did the Pendleton Act do for Civil Service reform?

_____

_____

_____

2.040 What happened to the National Bank under Andrew Jackson?

_____

_____

_____

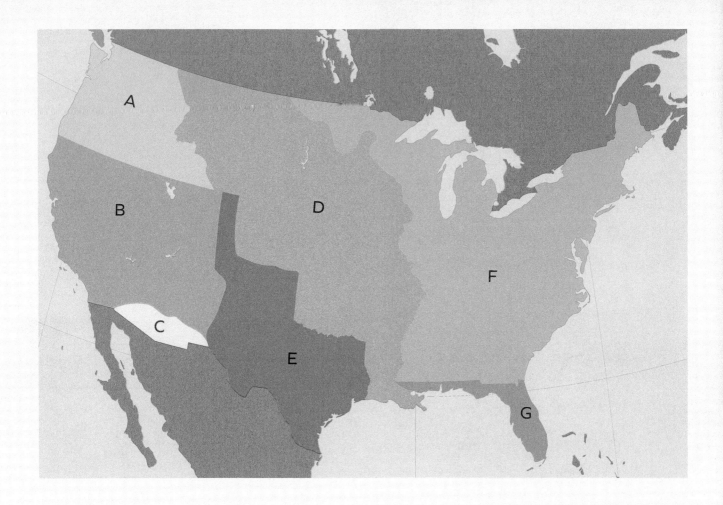

Using the map, give the letter for the named section (each answer, 2 points).

2.041 _____ Oregon Cession

2.042 _____ Louisiana Purchase

2.043 _____ United States in 1818

2.044 _____ Gadsden Purchase

2.045 _____ Mexican Cession

Teacher check: Initials _____

Score _____ Date _____

80
/
100

3. MODERN AMERICA (1930 - NEW MILLENNIUM)

This section will review the events of modern America, from 1930 until the present. It will cover the Great Depression, both World Wars, and the Cold War. It will also review some of the changes that came to the United States because of the Civil Rights Movement and the Vietnam War. Notice how much American history involves world history in this section. America is no longer an isolated nation. This review will complete your study of the history of the United States of America.

Objectives

Review the objective. When you have completed this section, you should be able to:

- Give a general overview of American history, recognizing important people, inventions, wars, and events.

Depression and War

The Great Depression. At its worst point, one out of four people could not get a job during the Great Depression. Banks and businesses closed, and people got poorer and poorer. The depression lasted from the Stock Market Crash in 1929 until 1942, after the U.S. entered World War II. President Herbert Hoover did not believe in using government money to help people, so people began to blame him for the depression. In 1932 Franklin Delano Roosevelt was elected president instead of Hoover.

Roosevelt (FDR) began to do all kinds of things to help people survive, to make jobs, to help businesses, and to change the laws so the depression could not happen again. He called his program the New Deal. The New Deal did not end the depression, but it did make things better and gave people hope. The New Deal kept going until it was no longer needed because manufacturing of supplies for World War II meant everyone could find a job.

The world goes to war. Several dictators came to power during the Great Depression. These dictators began to seize other nations, and the League of Nations was not able to stop them. The Japanese military government took Manchuria in northern China in 1931. Italy, under dictator Benito Mussolini, took Ethiopia in 1935. The most dangerous of these dictators was Adolf Hitler of Germany.

Hitler led the Nazi Party in Germany. He believed that Germans were a "master race" that should rule the world. He hated other races, especially Jews. He rebuilt Germany's military power and began his plan to get land for Germany. He took Austria and Czechoslovakia in 1938. The democracies of Europe tried to appease him by letting him have those lands, hoping he would not want more. Finally, in 1939, Hitler invaded Poland. France and Great Britain (the Allies) declared war. That was the beginning of World War II.

| Adolph Hitler

Hitler quickly conquered most of Europe, including France. Most of France was occupied by Germany. A small piece was left in the south to rule itself. It was called Vichy, France. Only Great Britain kept fighting. Under its Prime Minister, Winston Churchill, Britain refused to surrender in spite of heavy bombing. Hitler decided against invading Britain and in 1941 invaded the Soviet Union instead. While all this was happening, the U.S. was isolationist and refused to join the war.

The U.S. really wanted to stay neutral in World War II. However, people realized how dangerous Hitler and his allies were.(Germany, Italy, and Japan formed an alliance called the Axis Powers). The U.S., therefore, began to help the Allies, especially after Great Britain was left to fight alone. FDR set up Lend-Lease which gave Great Britain all the war supplies she needed. FDR and Churchill also wrote the Atlantic Charter that set out their goals for after the war, including a new organization of nations that could keep the peace.

The U.S. finally entered the war when Japan attacked Pearl Harbor, Hawaii on December 7, 1941. The attack was a complete surprise. All of the U.S. battleships in the harbor were sunk or heavily damaged. Over 2,000 Americans were killed. The navy's three large aircraft carriers were out at sea and were spared.

The United States was extremely angry about Pearl Harbor. Congress declared war the very next day. The whole country was suddenly and completely committed to war.

War in Europe. The U.S. quickly began to produce all the guns, tanks, jeeps, and supplies the Allies needed to win the war. Using planes, convoys, and sonar, the Allies were able to defeat the German submarines that tried to sink ships carrying supplies to Europe in the Battle of the Atlantic. At home, Americans had rationing and shortages of many new things, but were committed to winning the war.

| The workforce needed to prepare for war pulled the U.S. out of the Great Depression.

Hitler made a big mistake when he invaded the Soviet Union in 1941 without preparing for winter warfare. The cold Russian winter stopped his advance. Part of his army was captured at Stalingrad in 1943. This was the turning point of the war in Europe. In the meantime, the Allies, led by the Americans, invaded North Africa (November 1942) and Italy (July 1943) under the European commander, American General Dwight D. Eisenhower.

On June 6, 1944, the Allies invaded Normandy in France. It was called D-Day. The invasion succeeded, and by the next year the Allies were fighting their way into Germany. Hitler committed suicide before his nation surrendered on May 7, 1945. The victory allowed the Allies to find out about the millions of people, especially Jews, Hitler had killed in Europe in what was called the Holocaust.

War in the Pacific. Japan won an amazing series of victories after Pearl Harbor, capturing Hong Kong, Wake, Guam, Thailand, Singapore, northern New Guinea, and part of Burma. The Americans in the Philippines, under General Douglas MacArthur, held out until April and May of 1942 on the Bataan Peninsula and Corregidor Island. They finally surrendered, and many died on the "Bataan Death March" when they were forced to walk to prison camps. MacArthur was ordered to leave before the surrender and promised to return.

The Japanese tried to invade the southern half of New Guinea in May of 1942. They were stopped at the Battle of the Coral Sea, the first navy battle in which the ships never saw each other. A month later, the Japanese sailed into a trap when they attacked Midway Island. The U.S. had broken the Japanese code and knew they were coming. The Battle of Midway was a huge American victory and the turning point of the war in the Pacific.

The U.S. slowly retook the islands held by Japan, using a plan called island hopping. The Americans would skip the best protected islands, capture others, and use them as a base to attack other islands closer to Japan. On all of the islands, the Japanese men fought to the death, causing horrible casualties. However, by early summer of 1945, the Allies had captured islands just south of Japan and were ready to invade. However, the cost in men would have been so high that President Harry S. Truman chose another way.

The U.S. had developed an atomic bomb in a secret program code-named the Manhattan Project. It had exploded the first bomb in the desert of New Mexico in July of 1945. Truman, who became president when FDR died in April 1945 (after being elected president four times), decided to use the new weapon on Japan. Japan surrendered on September 2, 1945, after two cities, Hiroshima and Nagasaki, were destroyed by atomic bombs in August.

After the war, several of the Nazi leaders were tried in Nuremberg, Germany for crimes against humanity in the Holocaust. The charter for a new organization of nations called the United Nations was written in San Francisco at the end of the war. This time, the U.S. was a founding member, and the new headquarters was built in New York City. The U.S. was no longer isolationist.

| Mushroom cloud over Nagasaki

Name the item, person, place, or thing.

3.1 _____ FDR's program to end the Great Depression

3.2 _____ Event that started World War II

3.3 _____ Fraction of people out of work at the worst of the Great Depression

3.4 _____ Event that ended the Great Depression

3.5 _____ Germany, Italy, Japan alliance

3.6 _____ People especially hated by Adolf Hitler

3.7 _____ FDR and Churchill's plan for the end of the war

3.8 _____ Dictator of Italy

3.9 _____ Dictator of Germany

3.10 _____ Prime Minister of Great Britain

3.11 _____ Unoccupied part of France

3.12 _____ U.S. plan to give Great Britain and the Allies all the war supplies they needed

3.13 _____ Event that got the U.S. into the war

3.14 _____ Allies fought this battle to get supplies to Europe past German submarines

3.15 _____ Hitler's big mistake in Europe

3.16 _____ Turning point of the war in Europe

3.17 _____ The three invasions the Allies made in Europe

_____

_____

3.18 _____ Name for the invasion of Normandy

3.19 _____ The murder of millions of people, especially Jews, by the Nazis

3.20 _____ U.S. commander in the Philippines when Japan invaded

3.21 _____ Stopped Japan's invasion of southern New Guinea

3.22 _____ Turning point of the war in the Pacific

3.23 _____ U.S. plan in the Pacific

3.24 _____ U.S. program to build an atomic bomb

3.25 _____ U.S. president elected four times

3.26 _____ Organization of nations created at the end of World War II

3.27 _____ President who decided to use the atomic bomb on Japan

3.28 _____ Cities hit by atomic bombs

_____

Cold War

Communist threat. After World War II, the U.S. expected to work with its ally the Soviet Union. However, the Soviets were determined to force their form of government, Communism, on the nations they had invaded in eastern Europe. Communism is a type of government which owns everything, allows no freedom, and controls its people by lies. Eastern Europe was forced to become Communist after World War II. The line that divided free Europe from communist Europe was called the Iron Curtain.

Thus, after World War II, the world was divided into two main groups in a Cold War. Each group was led by one of the super powers. The U.S. led the Free World, the rich democracies of the west. The Soviet Union led the Communist Bloc. The Cold War was a war of ideas, alliances, and fear. It lasted from 1945 until 1989. The U.S. and U.S.S.R. never fought each other for fear of starting a nuclear war that might destroy everything on earth. However, they did help other people fight.

The U.S. did not become isolationist after World War II. The fear that Communists would take over Europe was too great. The U.S. acted in many ways to stop Communism. The Marshall Plan gave the countries of western Europe money to rebuild after the war. America also joined the North Atlantic Treaty Organization (NATO), an alliance set up to protect Europe.

Germany and Berlin were divided into four parts after the war. The British, U.S., and French parts became free West Germany. Communist East Germany came from the Soviet part. Berlin, inside East Germany, was also divided. In 1948 the Soviets tried to drive the free nations out of Berlin by blockading it. The Berlin Airlift supplied by plane all that West Berlin needed for a year. Later, in 1961, the East Germans would build the Berlin Wall around West Berlin to keep their people from escaping Communism.

In China, a civil war started again after World War II. Chiang Kai-shek, leader of the Nationalists and a U.S. ally, lost the war and fled to the island of Taiwan. Mao Zedong and his Communists won with Soviet help, making China a Communist nation in 1949. America said the government of Taiwan was the real government of China and gave them the Chinese seat at the United Nations until 1971.

| President Eisenhower (with Chiang Kai-shek) visiting Taiwan in 1960

In America, people were very afraid of Communism. The Soviet Union launched the first man-made satellite, Sputnik, in 1957. Fearful of having Communist power in space, the U.S. quickly built up its own space exploration, eventually putting the first man on the moon in 1969.

Americans were also afraid of Communist spies. Senator Joseph McCarthy made claims about spies in the government that made him popular and caused fear. McCarthy accused many people who lost their jobs even when he had no proof. He was finally censured for his actions after a hearing on TV showed him to be a lying bully.

Korean War. Communist North Korea invaded free South Korea in 1950. The United Nations sent an army to stop them, mainly from the United States, led by General Douglas MacArthur. MacArthur made a brilliant landing at Inchon, behind the North Koreans and drove them back, almost to China. Then, the Chinese joined the war and the two sides fought back to the old border between North and South, where they finally agreed to a ceasefire.

Crises. Several crises, or problems, made the Free World and Communist Bloc continue to distrust each other. The Soviets shot down a U-2 spy plane from the U.S. over their land in 1960. In 1959 Cuba, an island south of Florida, became Communist under Fidel Castro. An American-trained army of Cubans failed to overthrow him when they invaded at the Bay of Pigs in 1961. In 1962 the Cuban Missile Crisis occurred when the Soviets tried to put missiles in Cuba. President Kennedy blockaded the island, and the Soviets agreed not to send the missiles. Also, all over the world the U.S. would help one side in a war, and the U.S.S.R. would help the other.

| A U.S. blockade prevented the Soviets from sending nuclear missiles to Cuba.

Vietnam. Vietnam was divided into a Communist North and non-Communist South. The South was not democratic, but the U.S. helped it. A war began in 1957 when the southern Communists rebelled, with help from the North. The U.S. sent thousands of advisers at first. Then in 1964 Congress passed the Gulf of Tonkin Resolution which gave the president power to do whatever was needed to stop the Communists. President Lyndon Johnson sent in soldiers who were never able to defeat the Communists. In 1973 President Richard Nixon arranged a ceasefire and got the U.S. soldiers out of the country. In 1975 the North won the war and made Vietnam Communist. It was the longest and most controversial war in U.S. history.

Upheaval in America. African Americans did not have equal rights in 1950. They were segregated in schools, buses, public bathrooms, and other places. They also could not vote freely. This was changed by the Civil Rights Movement which began in 1955 with the Montgomery Bus Boycott. The boycott was led by Martin Luther King, Jr. who went on to lead the Civil Rights Movement all over the south. King and his supporters peacefully refused to obey segregation laws and protested against unequal treatment. Their efforts led to Black Americans finally being given the same legal rights as other Americans. King continued his work until he was assassinated in 1968.

All over America, young people in the 1960s and 1970s rebelled against old ideas of family, law, and religion. They protested to change things they did not like, such as pollution and laws that made drugs illegal. The most widespread protests were against the Vietnam War. The war was hated in America because many people believed the South Vietnamese government should not be defended. They also hated the cost of the war in money and men. Some young men refused to register for the draft or fled the country when they were drafted into the army. The protests sometimes became riots as the protesters fought with the police. Many Americans were afraid our nation would not survive all this anger.

The U.S. had four presidents between 1953 and 1973. Dwight Eisenhower (1953-61) was a war hero who did not change things much, except to start the American highway system. John Kennedy, however, wanted to change many things with his New Frontier. He started the Peace Corps and tried to get Civil Rights laws passed. He was assassinated in 1963. The new president, Lyndon Johnson (1963-69), was able to pass many of Kennedy's ideas, including the Civil Rights Act of 1964. Johnson also tried to end poverty in America with his "Great Society," but the huge cost of the Vietnam War left the government too short of money. Richard Nixon was elected in 1968, and he got America out of Vietnam. However, the war was so long and controversial that Americans distrusted their government more after that.

| In the 1970s, hippies promoted peace, sometimes called "flower power."

Complete these sentences.

3.29 _____ is a type of government which owns everything, allows no freedom, and controls its people by lies.

3.30 The _____ was the dividing line between free and communist Europe.

3.31 The _____ gave western Europe money to rebuild after World War II.

3.32 Americans supplied Berlin for a year by airplanes during the _____ _____ .

3.33 _____ was the United Nations commander in Korea.

3.34 The Chinese Nationalist leader, _____ , fled to the island of Taiwan while the communist leader, _____ , took over China in 1949.

3.35 The _____ was put up around West Berlin to keep East Germans from going through there to escape communism.

3.36 Senator _____ made accusations about communists in government and was censured by Congress for it.

3.37   The first man-made satellite was _____ launched by the

_____ in 1957.

3.38   In the _____ Crisis, the Soviets tried to put missiles

on an island just south of Florida.

3.39   The _____ War was the longest and most controversial

war in U.S. history.

3.40   The _____ Resolution gave the president power

to do whatever was needed to stop communism in Vietnam.

3.41   President _____ arranged a ceasefire in Vietnam and removed

the American soldiers in 1973.

3.42   Black Americans received the same legal rights as other Americans because of the

_____ .

3.43   The most widespread protests of the 1960s and 1970s were about the

_____ .

3.44   Young Americans in the 1960s _____ against laws, family,

and religion.

3.45   President _____ started the Peace Corps and was

assassinated in 1963.

3.46   President _____ lost his Great Society to the cost

of the Vietnam War.

3.47   President _____ was a war hero who started the

highway system.

3.48   The leader of the Civil Rights Movement was _____ ,

who began his work in 1955 at the _____ .

End of the Millennium

Fall of a president. President Richard Nixon changed the way America dealt with China and the U.S.S.R. He began discussions with communist China and became the first president to visit there. This alarmed the Soviets who needed western technology, so they also opened talks with the U.S. and allowed Nixon to visit them. The two sides signed SALT, the Strategic Arms Limitation Treaty, limiting the atomic arms race. This began a thaw in the Cold War that was called détente. It lasted until the Soviets invaded Afghanistan in 1979.

Watergate was a scandal that began in 1972. In June burglars hired by some of the president's aides broke into the Democratic Party headquarters in the Watergate complex. They were caught. Nixon was told and had his people cover up how they were involved. A long investigation proved this when Nixon was forced to release tapes he had made of the conversations in his office. Nixon, threatened with impeachment, became the first U.S. president to resign from office.

Gerald Ford had been appointed as vice president and became president when Nixon left. He was the only president appointed, not elected, to his post. He became very unpopular when he pardoned Nixon. He lost the 1976 election to Jimmy Carter. Carter won because he stressed that he was inexperienced and was new to the federal government.

America in the 1970s. The two biggest problems in America in the 1970s were inflation and the energy crisis. Inflation drove prices up quickly and was finally stopped by the Federal Reserve Board in 1979. The energy crisis was a time of shortage of oil which caused prices to rise and sometimes gasoline was hard to find. The high prices encouraged more production, which ended the shortages.

In 1978 President Jimmy Carter hosted Anwar Sadat, the president of Egypt, and Menachem Begin, the prime minister of Israel. They were trying to make peace. They stayed at the president's retreat at Camp David and wrote an agreement that was the basis for a peace treaty in 1979. The agreement in 1978 was called the Camp David Accords.

| Anwar Sadat (left), President Jimmy Carter (middle), and Menachem Begin (right)

In 1979 the American embassy in Iran was attacked by a mob. They were angry because the U.S. was allowing the old ruler of the country to visit America for medical care. The mob took 52 American diplomats as hostages. The Iranian government would not release them. They were held as prisoners for 444 days. They were finally released because Iran went to war with Iraq and needed money that was held in America. However, they were not released until Ronald Reagan became president in January of 1981.

While the Iran Hostage Crisis was going on, the Soviet Union invaded Afghanistan. This ended détente and hopes for the end of the Cold War. The Soviets were unable to conquer the nation, because of Islamic fighters who refused to surrender, and withdrew in 1988-89.

Rebuilding confidence. Ronald Reagan was elected president in 1980 because people had lost confidence in Jimmy Carter. Reagan opposed communism and reduced government control as well as taxes in America. He changed the direction of the government toward these ideas. It was called the Reagan revolution.

Reagan faced a number of problems in his eight years as president. Terrorists made several attacks on Americans including bombing a Marine barracks in Lebanon, killing about 200 servicemen. The Iran-Contra Affair was a scandal in which the president had sold weapons to Iran in the hopes of getting help for American hostages. The money was used to help the Contras of Nicaragua who were fighting the communist Sandinista government there. Congress had forbidden aid to the Contras, and several of Reagan's aides were arrested in the scandal. In 1983 Reagan invaded the island of Grenada in the Caribbean to overthrow the communist government there.

China began to move away from communism after Mao Zedong died in 1976. Under their new leader, Deng Xiaoping, businesses and farms were given back to the people. They were encouraged to make money. However, they were not allowed more freedom. When students protested for freedom in Tiananmen Square, Beijing, in 1989 they were attacked and driven out by the Chinese Army.

| The Chinese Army used tanks to control protesters in Tiananmen Square.

The Soviet Union began reforms, too, under Mikhail Gorbachev to rebuild businesses and allow more freedom of speech. Gorbachev met with President Reagan at several summits, and the two agreed to cut back the number of atomic bombs they had. Gorbachev also said he would no longer use the Soviet Army to protect communism in eastern Europe.

The year 1989 was called the miracle year. Knowing the Soviets would not stop them, people in eastern Europe protested against communism. Many of the communist governments in Europe ended that year. The Berlin Wall came down. It was the end of the Cold War.

Under President George H. W. Bush, the government had to pay billions of dollars to resolve the Savings and Loan Crisis in which many banks insured by the government failed. The U.S. also invaded Panama in 1989 to overthrow Manuel Noriega, a drug-smuggling military leader there. This, with the success in Grenada and in the Cold War, began to restore American confidence in the government and the military which had been damaged by the Vietnam War and Watergate.

After the Cold War. In 1990 Iraq's dictator, Saddam Hussein, invaded Kuwait to take over that nation's oil wealth. President George H. W. Bush organized a coalition to drive them out. The Persian Gulf War, led from Washington by General Colin Powell, was a huge success.

General Norman Schwarzkopf led the coalition army which at first protected Saudi Arabia from invasion (Operation Desert Shield) and then drove Iraq out of Kuwait (Operation Desert Storm). The coalition bombed Iraq and Kuwait for five weeks beginning in January of 1991. In February the coalition invaded, sweeping into Iraq north of the defenses along the Saudi-Kuwait border. Kuwait was freed in about 100 hours of fighting. America gained tremendous prestige.

| Saddam Hussein's army set fire to oil wells along their retreat from Kuwait.

In 1991 the communists in the Soviet Union tried to take over the government. Boris Yeltsin, the elected president of the Russian Republic (a republic was like a state in the U.S.) stopped them. At the end of the year, the Soviet Union dissolved into fifteen new countries. Russia took over the Soviet seat in the United Nations.

In America the government turned to other problems. Huge deficits in the 1980s were finally reduced in the 1990s by spending cuts and prosperity. The U.S. invaded Somalia under President George H. W. Bush in 1992 to protect the delivery of food to its starving people. The U.S. refused to get very involved in the wars in the country that used to be communist Yugoslavia. However, America did try bombing, negotiations, and peacekeeping troops to try to bring peace there. Under President Bill Clinton, the U.S. threatened to invade Haiti in 1994 to restore an elected government. The military government agreed to leave hours before the invasion. The U.S. also signed NAFTA, the North American Free Trade Agreement, in 1988 to create a free trade zone with Mexico, the U.S., and Canada. President Bill Clinton became the second president ever to be impeached when he lied under oath. He was acquitted in a trial in 1999.

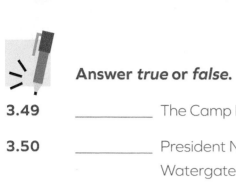

Answer *true* or *false*.

3.49 _____ The Camp David Accords were a basis for peace between Israel and Iran.

3.50 _____ President Nixon started Détente and resigned from office because of Watergate.

3.51 _____ SALT was a treaty for free trade.

3.52 _____ The Iran Hostage Crisis was when 52 American diplomats were held hostage for 444 days.

3.53 _____ The U.S. invaded Grenada to overthrow a communist government in 1983.

3.54 _____ The Soviet Union split into ten countries in 1993.

3.55 _____ Boris Yeltsin was the elected leader of Russia who stopped the communist takeover of the government in 1991.

3.56 _____ The U.S. invaded Panama in 1989 to overthrow the military leader, Manuel Noriega, who was smuggling drugs.

3.57 _____ China began to give its people back their businesses and farms after Mao's death in 1976.

3.58 _____ Détente ended when the Soviets invaded Afghanistan in 1979.

3.59 _____ Communism fell in Europe, and the Cold War ended in 1995.

3.60 _____ The Persian Gulf War was fought to drive Kuwait out of Saudi Arabia.

3.61 _____ Norman Schwarzkopf was the leader of the coalition army in the Persian Gulf War.

3.62 _____ Students who protested for freedom in Tiananmen Square were allowed to continue doing so by Deng Xiaoping.

3.63 _____ Mikhail Gorbachev and Saddam Hussein agreed to the Camp David Accords with Jimmy Carter's help.

3.64 _____ The Iran-Contra Affair was an attack by the Contras on the Iranian embassy in Nicaragua.

3.65 _____ Gerald Ford was elected president after Richard Nixon and refused to pardon him.

3.66 _____ The U.S. invaded Somalia in 1992 and threatened to invade Haiti in 1994.

3.67 _____ NAFTA includes the U.S., the Soviet Union and China.

3.68 _____ Inflation and deficits were big problems in America in the 1970s.

3.69 _____ Jimmy Carter was the second U.S. president to be impeached.

The New Millennium

September 11, 2001. The U.S. had not been immune* to terrorist strikes over the years. Most of the acts of terrorism had taken place overseas at military posts or places visited by Americans. Terrorism at home had come from Americans who attacked their own citizens. A September day in 2001 changed America's sense of security at home. Terrorists from the Al Qaeda terrorist organization hijacked four U.S. airplanes. They intended to use the planes as weapons against major American buildings. Two of the planes hit the twin towers of the World Trade Center in New York City. Another was flown into the Pentagon in Washington D.C. A fourth plane did not reach its target because the people on board the plane attempted to retake it from the hijackers. All aboard the fourth plane were killed when it crashed in Pennsylvania. At the end of the day, over 3000 Americans had died.

| Terrorist used planes as missiles and flew them into the World Trade Center in New York City.

* immune – protected or free from; had resistance to

In response to the attacks, President George W. Bush formed the Office of Homeland Security. This office was put in charge of keeping America safe from terrorism. Security in airports became stricter. America also worked to keep its borders more secure.

Afghanistan. The terrorists who attacked the U.S. were based in Afghanistan. Osama bin Laden led the Al Qaeda organization. The people of Afghanistan were ruled by the Taliban who were sympathetic to Osama bin Laden. The U.S. Army entered Afghanistan intent on finding bin Laden and driving out the terrorists. They also wanted to end the Taliban's control over the country. While bin Laden was not found, the government of the Taliban toppled. A new democratic form of government took its place.

Finally, in May 2011, bin Laden was killed in Pakistan by U.S. Navy Seals, ending a nearly decade-long search for him. In 2012, Afghanistan signed a partnership agreement with the U.S. that gave Afghan forces control over combat operations. By 2015, many of the U.S. troops had left Afghanistan, but a small population stayed to assist with long-term counter-terrorism efforts.

| U.S. soldiers in Iraq

Iraq. President George W. Bush ordered the invasion of Iraq in 2003. Saddam Hussein was a powerful dictator who had cruelly ruled his people for decades. The U.S. and others feared that he was hiding powerful weapons. The U.S. and other nations agreed to invade Iraq and remove him from power. They were successful in doing so. Saddam Hussein fled Baghdad and hid. He was eventually found, tried by the Iraqi people and put to death for his crimes.

The transition from a dictatorship to a democracy in Iraq was not smooth and conflict continued. The military of the U.S. trained an Iraqi police force, a measure designed to help keep order amid civil disorder. The withdrawal of U.S. troops from Iraq began in 2007 and was essentially completed the end of 2011, marking the end of the Iraq War.

In 2014, however, the U.S. initiated a campaign against Islamist extremist terrorist group, ISIL, operating in Syria and Iraq. The U.S. increased the presence of soldiers in Iraq in an effort to aid the anti-ISIL forces engaged in the Iraqi Civil War.

Barack Obama. In 2008 Barack Obama was elected 44th president of the United States. He was the first African-American to be elected to office. His historic inauguration was viewed by millions of people around the world. During his inauguration address he said, "On this day, we gather because we have chosen hope over fear, unity of purpose over conflict and discord."

During his first term, Obama focused his efforts on mitigating the global financial crisis, reforming healthcare through new legislation, and continuing the 2007 transition of U.S. troops out of Iraq. He also made a historic appointment in Sonia Sotomayor who became the first Hispanic American to serve on the Supreme Court.

During his second term, President Obama turned his attention to combating climate change, which included signing an international climate agreement; restoring relations with Iran and Cuba, and managing the withdrawal of U.S. troops in Afghanistan. One of his most notable feats was implementing the Affordable Care Act, a federal statute enacted by Congress designed to overhaul and expand medical coverage to the uninsured. The ACA drew support, but was also met with challenges and opposition. Upon the completion of his second term, Obama's presidency came to an end in January 2017.

Financial Crisis of 2008. In September 2008, widespread failure of U.S. financial institutions led to the worst financial crisis since the Great Depression. The crisis was caused by a number of factors, primarily the result of people nationwide purchasing homes that they later could not afford. Banks stopped lending money to each other and loans could not be repaid. National governments had to bail out banks to prevent their total collapse.

As a result, the banking crisis led to a global economic recession. International trade slowed, unemployment was pervasive, and stock and housing markets suffered. It wasn't until late 2012 that the economy started to improve.

Donald Trump. In January 2017, Donald Trump was inaugurated as 45th president of the United States. A businessman from New York City, Trump is the only president without prior political or military office. President Trump's major platforms focused on economic reform and immigration.

 Suggested Research Project.

This section has only covered a few of the major events in U.S. history since the start of the 21st century. Conduct additional research using a mix of print and online sources to learn about other significant events. Prepare a 750-word report that highlights and summarizes at least three important historical events that you found in your research.

Answer *true* or *false*.

3.70 _____ The U.S. had never experienced a terrorist attack before September 11, 2001.

3.71 _____ The September 11 terrorists used airplanes as weapons.

3.72 _____ Osama bin Laden headed the Al Qaeda terrorist group.

3.73 _____ Osama bin Laden was also the dictator of Iraq.

3.74 _____ President Obama was the first African-American president of the U.S.

3.75 _____ The U.S. decided against invading Iraq and removing Saddam Hussein from power.

Before you take this last Self Test, you may want to do one or more of these self checks.

1. _____ Read the objectives. See if you can do them.

2. _____ Restudy the material related to any objectives that you cannot do.

3. _____ Use the **SQ3R** study procedure to review the material:

    a. **S**can the sections.

    b. **Q**uestion yourself.

    c. **R**ead to answer your questions.

    d. **R**ecite the answers to yourself.

    e. **R**eview areas you did not understand.

4. _____ Review all vocabulary, activities, and Self Tests, writing a correct answer for every wrong answer.

SELF TEST 3

Match these people (each answer, 2 points).

3.01	_____ President, used the atomic bomb in World War II	a. Franklin Roosevelt
		b. Adolf Hitler
3.02	_____ President, organized the coalition that fought the Persian Gulf War	c. Dwight Eisenhower
		d. Winston Churchill
3.03	_____ Army commander in the Persian Gulf War	e. Mikhail Gorbachev
		f. Mao Zedong
3.04	_____ Civil Rights leader, assassinated	g. Harry Truman
3.05	_____ Chinese communist leader	h. Douglas MacArthur
3.06	_____ Nazi dictator of Germany	i. Martin Luther King, Jr.
3.07	_____ Only appointed president	j. Lyndon Johnson
3.08	_____ President during most of World War II, elected four times, used federal money to try and end the Great Depression	k. Richard Nixon
		l. George H. W. Bush
		m. Ronald Reagan
		n. Norman Schwarzkopf
		o. Gerald Ford

3.09 _____ American general, lost the Philippines in World War II, led U.N. Army in Korea

3.010 _____ Last president of the U.S.S.R., his reforms ended communism there

3.011 _____ First president to visit China and the U.S.S.R., only one to resign from office

3.012 _____ Prime minister of Britain, World War II

3.013 _____ President, wanted to fight communism and reduce the power of the government

3.014 _____ Commander of Allied forces in Europe in World War II, expanded the highway system as president

3.015 _____ President, lost his War on Poverty to the Vietnam War

Name the place, event, war, or thing (each answer, 3 points).

3.016 _____ Began with the Stock Market Crash in 1929, ended with World War II

3.017 _____ The murder of millions of people, especially Jews, during World War II by the Nazis

3.018 _____ Place attacked in 1941, got the U.S. into World War II

3.019 _____ The longest, most controversial war in U.S. history people protested against it in the 1960s and early 70s

3.020 _____ Dividing line between free and communist Europe after World War II

3.021 _____ War of ideas, alliances, and fear between the U.S. and the U.S.S.R. from 1945 to 1989

3.022 _____ 52 American diplomats were held hostage 444 days from 1979 to 1981

3.023 _____ Nation invaded by Iraq in the Persian Gulf War

3.024 _____ The Soviets invaded this nation in 1979 ending Détente, they left in 1988-89

3.025 _____ Place invaded on D-Day in World War II

3.026 _____ Country where Osama bin Laden's Al Qaeda was based

3.027 _____ This man was the dictator of Iraq who was eventually tried and killed for his crimes

3.028 _____ He became the first African-American president of the United States

Answer *true* or *false* (each answer, 2 points).

3.029 _____ Communism collapsed in Europe in 1989.

3.030 _____ Jimmy Carter was a president who invaded Grenada, Haiti, and Panama.

3.031 _____ The first man-made satellite was Sputnik launched by the Soviet Union.

3.032 _____ The U.S. blockaded Cuba in the Cuban Missile Crisis.

3.033 _____ The students that protested for freedom in Tiananmen Square were attacked by the Chinese Army.

3.034 _____ The Persian Gulf War was an embarrassing failure for the United States.

3.035 _____ Bill Clinton and Andrew Johnson were the only presidents impeached.

3.036 _____ Federal deficits came down in the 1990s due to spending cuts and prosperity.

3.037 _____ The Korean War was fought by the United Nations and did not result in the country being united again.

3.038 _____ The turning point of World War II in Pacific was at Midway.

Match these items (each answer, 2 points).

3.039 _____ Big problem in the 1970s, ended by the Federal Reserve Board

3.040 _____ Scandal, cover-up after a burglary, the president resigned

3.041 _____ Plan by the president to give the Allies all they needed to win World War II

3.042 _____ Agreement between Anwar Sadat and Menachem Begin with Jimmy Carter's help for peace between Egypt and Israel

3.043 _____ Created a free trade zone between the U.S., Canada, and Mexico

3.044 _____ Franklin Roosevelt's plan to end the Great Depression

a. Lend-Lease

b. New Deal

c. Gulf of Tonkin

d. Island Hopping

e. Berlin Wall

f. Camp David Accords

g. SALT

h. Watergate

i. inflation

j. NAFTA

3.045 _____ Barrier around a city to keep communist East Germans from escaping to freedom

3.046 _____ American strategy to retake the land captured by Japan in World War II

3.047 _____ Resolution that gave the president the power to do whatever was needed to defeat the communists in Vietnam

3.048 _____ Treaty to reduce atomic weapons

Teacher check:

Score _____

Initials _____

Date _____

87 / 109

Before you take the LIFEPAC Test, you may want to do one or more of these self checks.

1. _____ Read the objectives. See if you can do them.
2. _____ Restudy the material related to any objectives that you cannot do.
3. _____ Use the **SQ3R** study procedure to review the material.
4. _____ Review activities, Self Tests, and LIFEPAC vocabulary words.
5. _____ Restudy areas of weakness indicated by the last Self Test.

NOTES

HISTORY & GEOGRAPHY 501
A NEW WORLD

Author:
Theresa K. Buskey, J.D.

Editor:
Alan Christopherson, M.S.

Media Credits:
Page 3: © Photodisc, Thinkstock; **5:** © Willard, iStock, Thinkstock; **6:** © lightphoto, iStock, Thinkstock; **8:** © MR1805, iStock, Thinkstock; **9:** © Mulecan, iStock, Thinkstock; **11:** © Tony Baggett, iStock, Thinkstock; **12, 14, 29, 34, 48, 57 :** © Photos.com, Thinkstock; **15:** © Dorling Kindersley, Thinkstock; **20:** © yerfdog, iStock, Thinkstock; **25:** © ziggymaj, iStock, Thinkstock; **26:** © Brian Swartz, iStock, Thinkstock; **27:** © Oleksiy Khmyz, iStock, Thinkstock; **31:** © stocksnapper, iStock, Thinkstock; **35:** © Elisa Frank, iStock, Thinkstock; **38:** © Tim Markley, iStock,Thinkstock; **39:** © leekris, iStock, Thinkstock; **45:** © larryhw, iStock, Thinkstock; **47:** © Briana May, iStock, Thinkstock; **54:** © Georgios Kollidas, iStock, Thinkstock, **58:** © trekandshoot, iStock, Thinkstock; **59:** © Don Croswhite, iStock, Thinkstock; **60:** © Brian Behunin, iStock, Thinkstock; **61:** © Susan Law Cain, iStock, Thinkstock.

All maps in this book © Map Resources, unless otherwise stated.

Alpha Omega
PUBLICATIONS

804 N. 2nd Ave. E.
Rock Rapids, IA 51246-1759

A NEW WORLD

This year you will learn the story, the history, of our nation, the United States of America. You will learn how it was created, how it survived, what people led it and what it has accomplished in the world. It is an amazing story of a nation led by the hand of God. It is also your story. God created you to be an American and to do your part in the history of your nation. When you grow up you will become a voting citizen, a government employee, or maybe even an elected official. Learn the history of your nation so you can better understand your place in America.

The origin of something is its beginning or source. This LIFEPAC® will teach you about the origins of the United States of America. It will teach you about the men who came from Europe, explored this land, and stayed to build their lives here. You will learn about how they formed thirteen colonies under the control of Great Britain. When Britain began to rule unfairly, the colonies formed their own nation, the United States.

Objectives

Read these objectives. The objectives tell you what you will be able to do when you have successfully completed this LIFEPAC. Each section will list according to the numbers below what objectives will be met in that section. When you have finished this LIFEPAC, you should be able to:

1. Name the explorers who were important in American history and what they explored.
2. Name the nations that claimed land in America and what they claimed.
3. Describe how each of the British colonies were founded and by whom.
4. Describe what the British colonies were like before the Revolution.
5. Describe the French and Indian War and why it changed Britain's thinking about its American colonies.
6. Describe the conflicts with Britain that led the Americans to revolt.
7. Describe the beginning of the Revolutionary War and the birth of the United States of America.

1. EUROPEAN EXPLORERS

The culture of the United States and most of its people came from Europe. You read last year about the European sailors who explored our earth and mapped it. In this section, you will learn about those who did this work in North America, our continent.

Four nations explored and claimed land in what is today the United States. They were: Spain, France, the Netherlands, and England. Each nation claimed a portion of land and started colonies there to protect it. Eventually, England would take over both the Dutch and the French claims. The Spanish colonies would be taken by the United States years later.

This section will teach you about these nations and their explorers. You will learn what parts of America they claimed and how they settled it. This was the very beginning of the events that changed America from a wilderness, which was home to scattered Native American tribes, into a powerful, united nation.

Objectives

Review these objectives. When you have completed this section, you should be able to:

1. Name the explorers who were important in American history and what they explored.
2. Name the nations that claimed land in America and what they claimed.

Vocabulary

Study these new words. Learning the meanings of these words is a good study habit and will improve your understanding of this LIFEPAC.

noblemen (nō′ bəl men). Men who have high social standing by birth, rank, or title.

Scandinavia (skan′ də nā vē ə). A region in northwestern Europe that includes Norway, Sweden, Denmark, and sometimes Finland and Iceland.

*Note: All vocabulary words in this LIFEPAC appear in **boldface** print the first time they are used. If you are unsure of the meaning when you are reading, study the definitions given.*

Pronunciation Key: hat, āge, cãre, fär; let, ēqual, tėrm; it, īce; hot, ōpen, ôrder; oil; out; cup, pu̇t, rüle; child; long; thin; /ŦH/ for then; /zh/ for measure; /u/ or /ə/ represents /a/ in about, /e/ in taken, /i/ in pencil, /o/ in lemon, and /u/ in circus.

| Viking long house in Canada

The Discovery of North America

Native Americans. The first people to discover America did so long before the Europeans began to explore. They were people from Asia who moved east from Babel, after God confused the languages. (Genesis 11:1-9). After many years of spreading east, some of these people crossed the Bering Sea on the ice or on a piece of land that is no longer there. These people settled the continents of North and South America. They became the many Indian or Native American tribes that still exist today. The Iroquois, Cherokee, Navajo, Apache, and Sioux people are some of the descendants of these first settlers.

Vikings. The Vikings were great sailors and pirates from **Scandinavia**. From about A.D. 700 to 1100 they raided all over Europe to steal treasures and take slaves. Their long wooden boats were fast and sturdy. They were able to travel throughout Europe and even into the vast Atlantic Ocean.

These Vikings explored the islands west of Europe. They colonized (sent people to live on) the island of Iceland northwest of Europe in about A.D. 870. From Iceland, they discovered the island of Greenland further west. A man named Eric the Red led people to colonize that island in about A.D. 985. One ship's crew while trying to reach Greenland sailed too far, and became the very first Europeans to see North America.

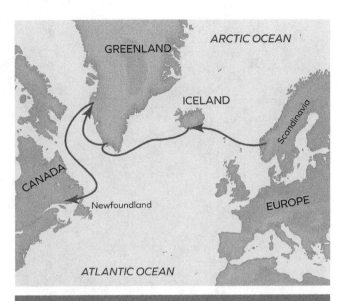

ABOUT DATES

We date things by whether they happened before or after the birth of Jesus.

Something that happened before His birth is dated B.C. (**B**efore **C**hrist).

Something that happened after His birth is dated A.D. (**A**nno **D**omini–Latin for "In the Year of Our Lord").

So, David became king of Israel in about 1000 B.C. (a thousand years before Jesus was born). Leif Ericson landed in America in about A.D. 1000 (a thousand years after Jesus was born).

B.C. is written after the date, but A.D. is written in front of it. If there are no letters with a date, it is A.D.

Eric the Red's son, Leif Ericson, led the first voyage to explore this new land in about A.D. 1000. He and his men probably landed in what is now Canada. They stayed one winter. Other Vikings followed them and tried to colonize the new lands. However, all the colonies were eventually abandoned, possibly because of attacks by the Indians. Icelandic sagas (stories) recorded Leif Ericson's journey, but the rest of Europe knew nothing about it. It would be almost 500 years before Europeans returned to America.

| Portuguese caravel

Trade. In the year 1400, the people of Europe knew very little about the world. They knew about Europe, the northern part of Africa and most of Asia (except for the far north). Antarctica and Australia were unknown. America was forgotten, except in the sagas of Iceland. However, the Europeans wanted to know more for a very important reason, spices!

Spices for food were very valuable in Europe in 1400. They were often worth their weight in gold. They came from the southeastern part of Asia (called the Far East or Spice Islands). The trade routes to get the spices from the Far East to Europe involved traveling over land and sea. The trips took a long time and were very expensive.

Europeans began to look for an all-water route to Asia in about 1400. Such a route would allow them to avoid the dangerous and expensive land crossings. They would be safer from thieves who attacked the caravans. They could send their own ships, fill them with spices and return on the open sea without having to pay tolls to anyone. Such a route would bring great wealth to the men and nations that used it.

Henry the Navigator, a Portuguese prince, began the exploration of the earth to find a water route to Asia. As you learned in LIFEPAC 401, he planned very carefully. He set up a school of navigation in his homeland to train sea captains and sailors. He organized voyages along the coast of Africa to explore, map, and search for a water route to Asia.

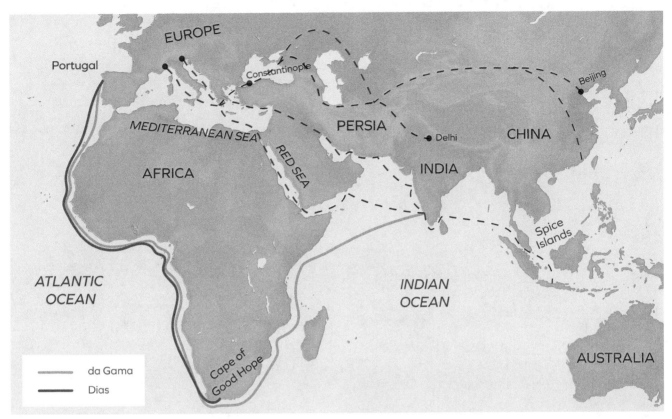

| Dias and da Gama routes to India

Prince Henry's ships began sailing down the
west coast of Africa in about 1430. Each
ship went further than the last one before
returning to Portugal. In 1488, a Portuguese
ship under the command of Bartholomeu Dias
sailed around the Cape of Good Hope, the
bottom of Africa. Just ten years later, another
Portuguese captain, Vasco da Gama, sailed

around Africa to India and back to Portugal. A water route to the Far East had been found!

The new route brought changes to Europe. Spices became cheaper and more plentiful.
Portugal and its merchants grew rich from the trade with the Far East. Portugal protected its
new wealth by setting up forts along the coast of Africa to make sure other nations did not
trade along "their" route. Other nations had already begun to search for their own route east.

Since most educated people knew the world was a sphere, several thought of sailing west,
around the world to reach Asia. But, no one was certain how far west a ship would have to sail
to get there. Ships usually sailed along coastlines. Sailing out into the open ocean, without any
promise of land nearby was a frightening thought. Moreover, no one knew what dangers or
monsters lay out away from land. It would take a brave and determined man to face such a
great unknown.

Choose the letter(s) that are true for each item or person.
Use all of the lettered choices.

1.1 _____ Native Americans

1.2 _____ Eric the Red

1.3 _____ Leif Ericson

1.4 _____ Henry the Navigator

1.5 _____ spices

1.6 _____ Vikings (as a group)

1.7 _____ B.C.

1.8 _____ A.D.

1.9 _____ Bartholomeu Dias

1.10 _____ Vasco da Gama

1.11 _____ Portugal

a. Before Christ

b. led people to colonize Greenland

c. colonized Iceland

d. Portuguese prince

e. what Europeans wanted from the Far East

f. first people to discover America

g. "In the Year of Our Lord"

h. first European to sail around the bottom of Africa

i. set up forts along the African coast to protect trade route

j. reached Europe by a difficult land and sea route in 1400

k. *Anno Domini*

l. nation that controlled the first all-water route to Asia

m. founded a navigation school

n. first European to sail to Asia around Africa

o. first European to reach America

p. crossed the Bering Sea

q. pirates and expert sailors

r. recorded the discovery of America in sagas

Columbus. The man who finally had the courage to try sailing west to Asia was Christopher Columbus. Columbus was an experienced Italian sailor. He was a very proud man who believed God was guiding him to do great things. He made two important mistakes in planning this voyage. He thought Asia was much closer to Europe than it really is and he did not know America was in the way. In spite of the dangers and the unknown, Columbus still dared to try this trip.

The king of Portugal would not give Columbus ships for the adventure and neither would the rulers of France or England. However, after many years of waiting, the rulers of Spain, Ferdinand and Isabella, agreed to financially support the voyage. They gave Columbus three ships, the *Niña*, the *Pinta* and the *Santa Maria*. The ships sailed from Spain in 1492. You can remember that date with the rhyme:

*In fourteen hundred and ninety-two
Columbus sailed the ocean blue!*

| Christopher Columbus with King Ferdinand and Queen Isabella of Spain

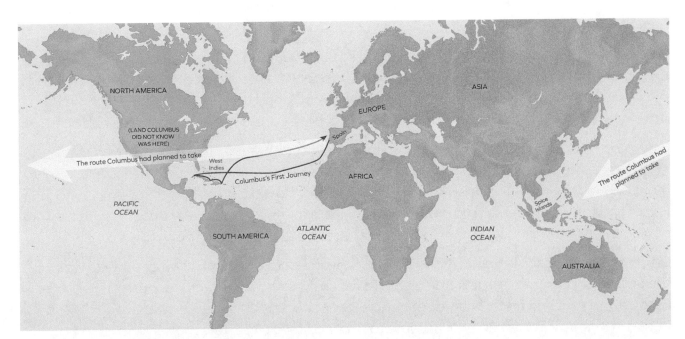

| The route Columbus planned to take

It was a long, difficult voyage for the men on the three ships. The sailors were ignorant, superstitious men. A few were afraid of falling off the edge of the earth or running into monsters. More practical men noticed that the wind that pushed the ships was only blowing west. How could they ever get home against the wind? The men became angry and threatening when they failed to reach land as quickly as Columbus said they would. Finally, in mid-October, 1492, after more than a month at sea, the adventurers spotted land!

On October 12, 1492, Columbus landed on one of the islands of the Caribbean Sea. He named the island *San Salvador* (Holy Savior). He believed he was in the Indies Islands southeast of the Asian mainland. He called the natives he met "Indians;" the name stuck even after his mistake was discovered. The archipelago was eventually called the "West Indies" to distinguish them from those in Asia.

| Columbus strides ashore

Columbus searched hard for the trading cities of Asia. He was *sure* they were nearby. Instead, all he found were peaceful Indians and beautiful islands. Finally, in January 1493, Columbus gave up the search and returned to Spain with what he had: some gold trinkets, plants, animals and a few captured Indians.

He returned to a hero's welcome. The king and queen believed he had found a new route to the riches of Asia. Another voyage was quickly arranged to set up Spanish colonies and protect the new route. On this second voyage, Columbus established the first European colony in the Americas, Isabela, on the island of Hispaniola. But, he still could not find the spices and cities!

Columbus made two more voyages to America, for a total of four. He explored much of the West Indies, the coast of Central America and even briefly reached South America. He fought more and more with the Spanish colonists in America who did not like him or his ways. King Ferdinand (after Queen Isabella died) would not let him keep the powers and privileges he had been promised. Columbus died in Spain in 1506 still believing he had reached Asia.

Columbus was a daring man to make that first voyage across the unknown ocean. He was not the first person, or even the first European, to reach America. However, because of his bravery, Europe and America finally knew about each other and, this time, the discovery would not be buried in legends. Europeans would come to America to explore, to conquer, and to settle. What Columbus began would one day result in a nation called the United States.

Complete these sentences.

1.12   Ferdinand and Isabella, rulers of _____ agreed to finance Columbus' voyage.

1.13   Columbus first landed on an island he named _____ in October

of _____ .

1.14   The two mistakes Columbus made were thinking _____ was closer

to Europe and not knowing _____ was in the way.

1.15   The archipelago where Columbus first landed was named the _____ .

1.16   The first European colony in the Americas was _____ on the

island of _____ .

1.17   Columbus believed he had sailed to _____ .

1.18   The ships on Columbus' first voyage were the _____ , the

_____ and the _____ .

1.19   Columbus sailed to America a total of _____ times.

Spanish Explorers

Spain moved quickly to secure the new lands Columbus had found. Many Spanish **noblemen** came to the new lands hoping to become rich. They conquered the Indians and stole their wealth. Spain rapidly became a very rich nation because of the gold and silver in Mexico and South America. The Spanish *conquistadors* (conquerors) greedily searched for more wealth and mapped the land as they went. Whenever they explored an area they claimed the land for Spain. Their explorations gradually proved that this was not Asia, but a "New World." Several of these men were important to American history.

Ponce de León. Ponce de León was a *conquistador* who came to America with Columbus on his second voyage. He heard a legend about a "Fountain of Youth" that would keep people who drank from it forever young. He believed it was on a peninsula north of the West Indies. He explored the peninsula, claiming it for Spain in 1513. He named the land *Florida* (flowery), but he never found his fountain. He tried to colonize Florida, but was driven out by hostile Indians.

Magellan. In 1519, a Portuguese captain named Ferdinand Magellan set out from Spain on a daring quest. He and his five ships were going to try to sail <u>all the way around the world!</u> Spain was becoming more and more certain that America was not Asia. A *conquistador* named Balboa had crossed the Isthmus of Panama in 1513 and seen the wide ocean on the other side. However, the rulers of Spain still had no idea how much further a ship had to go to reach Asia. If the New World and Asia were close together, it would still be a good trade route. Magellan was going to find out once and for all.

| A portrait of Magellan

He and his men sailed south along the coast of South America searching everywhere for a way across or around the continent. They finally reached the southern end of it after almost a year. With great difficulty his three remaining ships sailed through the passage (named the Straits of Magellan) to the ocean beyond. The passage was stormy but the ocean on the other side was very calm. So, Magellan named it *Pacific*, which means peaceful.

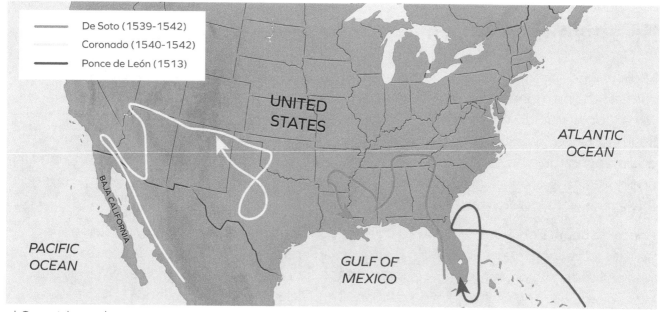

De Soto (1539-1542)
Coronado (1540-1542)
Ponce de León (1513)

UNITED STATES

ATLANTIC OCEAN

BAJA CALIFORNIA

PACIFIC OCEAN

GULF OF MEXICO

| Spanish explorers map

Magellan and his men had no idea how big the Pacific Ocean was. It is the biggest ocean in the world! They thought they could sail a just little way to Asia. In fact, they sailed for almost <u>100 days</u> without finding any place to get water or food. They got so hungry they ate leather and rats. However, they eventually reached Asia and stopped to recover on the Philippine Islands. There, Magellan was killed. Only one ship, the *Victoria*, returned to Spain around Africa with eighteen men aboard.

Magellan's voyage (1519-1522) proved that the New World was a separate land, far from Asia. It also proved that the earth was huge. Magellan's route, around the southern end of South America, was far too long and dangerous for normal trade. From that time on, Europeans began to search for a shortcut through America to Asia. They also began to look for ways to make money from the new lands. Very few Europeans cared that there were already people, Native Americans, living there. They thought the land was theirs to take, and they took it.

De Soto and Coronado. Two other conquistadors explored to the north, into what is now the United States. Hernando De Soto discovered the Mississippi River and explored parts of land between Florida and the river in 1538. Francisco Coronado went even further during the time between 1540 and 1542. After hearing a story about seven cities of gold, he explored the area of Arizona, New Mexico, and Texas. His men discovered the Grand Canyon, the Rio Grande Valley, and the pueblo towns of the local Native Americans, but no cities of gold.

The explorers did not find great riches in the north. So, they concentrated on building colonies in South America, the Caribbean, and Mexico. They left the north open for other nations to explore and claim. They did, however, build a few cities in the southern part of the United States, including the very first permanent European settlement. That was the city of St. Augustine, Florida, founded by the Spanish in 1565.

| A conquistador

Match these people with their description.

1.20 _____ Hernando De Soto

1.21 _____ Ponce de León

1.22 _____ Ferdinand Magellan

1.23 _____ St. Augustine, Florida

1.24 _____ *conquistadors*

1.25 _____ Francisco Coronado

a. Led the first voyage around the world

b. Explored between Florida and the Mississippi River

c. Explored and named Florida, looking for the Fountain of Youth

d. Spanish noblemen who came to America to conquer and get rich

e. First European settlement in the U.S.

f. Explored Arizona, New Mexico & Texas

New France

Other nations that set up colonies in America usually did it many years after Spain. An English explorer, John Cabot, had discovered the Grand Banks, a wonderful fishing area near Canada just a few years after Columbus. Many nations sent their fleets there to fish. These ships came only for the fishing season and then left.

France was one nation that fished the Grand Banks. However, the French king saw how wealthy Spain was becoming in America and he hoped to also find a trade route through North America to Asia. (This route was called the *Northwest Passage* because it went north and west of Europe to Asia. Hundreds of explorers searched all over North America for it. It does exist, north of Canada, but it is so far north and so full of ice it could never be a good trade route.) The French king decided to start by sponsoring the exploration of the large gulf west of the Grand Banks.

Cartier. The king sent Jacques Cartier to do the work beginning in 1534. Cartier explored the gulf and found a huge river that came into it in the west. He named the river the St. Lawrence. Working over several years, Cartier explored down the river as far as what is now the city of Montreal, where river rapids stopped him. He and his men managed to stay in Canada during the harsh winter, but they were not able to start a colony.

Champlain. The man who finally founded a French colony in Canada was Samuel de Champlain. He earned the title the "Father of New France" for his hard work. He began exploring in 1603, looking for the Northwest Passage. He followed the St. Lawrence all the way to its source at Lake Ontario. He explored the eastern end of that lake. He followed a tributary of the St. Lawrence (the Ottawa) west and then set out on foot when it turned north. He found and explored the northeast part of Lake Huron. He also explored Upstate New York and discovered Lake Champlain, which he named after himself.

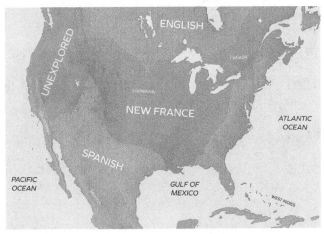

| European possessions in North America

Champlain established the city of Quebec in 1608. He made friends with the nearby Algonquin Indians to help protect the new settlement. The Algonquin's enemies, the Iroquois, became enemies of the French. Later on, these powerful people would become allies of the British and would fight against the French.

Furs. New France became a profitable colony because of the trade in furs. Fur was very popular and valuable in Europe. The French settlers spread out and set up trading forts all over their land to trade with the Indians for furs. They explored far and wide to find new areas to get furs. Their forts were far apart and very few Frenchmen lived there. Thus, they held a large area of land with only a few people.

Mississippi. New France spread out along the St. Lawrence and the Great Lakes. In time, the French colonists heard from the Indians about a great river south of the lakes called the Mississippi. Still hoping for a passage west to Asia, the French set out to find and explore the river.

The first expedition down the river was led by two men. Louis Jolliet was a fur trader/explorer. Jacques Marquette was a Catholic priest (France was a Catholic nation). They set out from Lake Michigan in 1673. They found the river and followed it south using canoes, which the French used a great deal in their explorations. They followed the river south to Arkansas. Then, realizing the river went south into Spanish territory, they turned back.

Another Frenchmen, Sieur de La Salle, set off down the river in 1682. He explored all the way down to the river's mouth in the Gulf of Mexico. He claimed all the land drained by the river for France, all of the Mississippi River basin from the Rocky Mountains to the Appalachians! That is the *entire* center part of the United States. He named the land Louisiana after the king of France. New France now spread out around the St. Lawrence, the Great Lakes, and the Mississippi River.

The French quickly built forts along the rivers to protect their claim. There were no roads, so rivers were the only safe, fast way to travel. As long as the French controlled the rivers and waterways, no one could move into their lands. They started the cities of New Orleans, Detroit and Mobile among many others.

Complete these sentences.

1.26   The passage through or around America to Asia was called the

_____ Passage.

1.27   La Salle claimed all the land drained by the _____ River.

1.28   Champlain became friends with the _____ Indians but enemies

of the _____ .

1.29   The first French colony in America was the city of _____ .

1.30   _____ was the "Father of New France."

1.31   La Salle named the land he claimed for France _____ .

1.32   New France became profitable by trading in _____ .

Find and mark these items on the map.

1.33   Quebec, Montreal, and New Orleans

1.34   Draw arrows to show the area explored by these men:

a. Cartier

b. Champlain

c. Marquette and Jolliet

d. La Salle

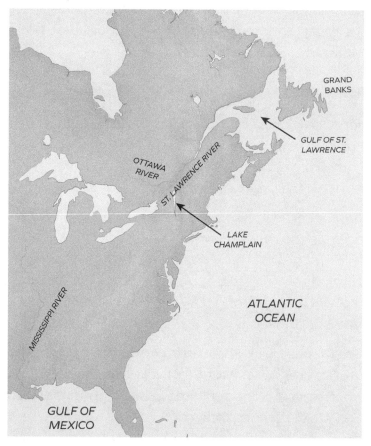

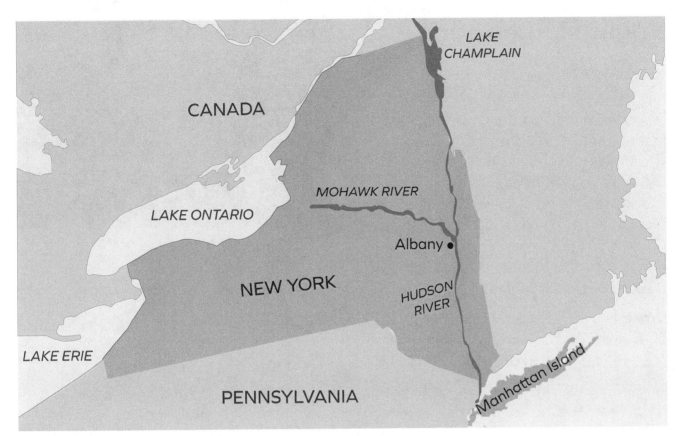

| New Netherlands

New Netherlands

The Dutch East India Company was a business in the Netherlands that wanted to trade with Asia. In 1609, they hired an experienced English sailor named Henry Hudson to find a trade route for them. He went to America hoping to find the Northwest Passage.

He and his crew explored along the east coast of the United States between the Carolinas and Canada. Hudson was delighted when he found a large river that ran deep into the wild land. He followed the river for miles, but it only continued north, never turning west toward Asia. He eventually gave up and returned to the Netherlands. His explorations gave the Dutch a claim to New York around what was named the Hudson River.

The Dutch *West* India Company was organized to use the new lands. They sent families to settle the land, to farm, and to trade for furs. They founded the city of Albany up the river. They also purchased the island of Manhattan in the excellent harbor at the river's mouth. They paid the local Indians about $24 worth of trade goods for it. There they founded the city of New Amsterdam.

The colony grew slowly, but steadily. Over the years the British built colonies north and south of New Netherlands. Eventually, the British would take over New Netherlands, renaming it New York.

English Exploration

| Sir Francis Drake

Cabot. England had many problems during the 1500s and did only a little exploring in America. John Cabot sailed to America for England just five years after Columbus' first voyage. He explored along the east coast of Canada and discovered the Grand Banks fishing area. He claimed the fish were so thick there that they could be scooped up in a bucket! He may also have explored down the east coast of the United States. He claimed the land he found for England, but nothing was done to protect the claim for many years.

Drake. Sir Francis Drake was an English *sea dog*. During this time Spain and England were bitter enemies. The sea dogs were men who attacked Spanish ships and cities, bringing captured treasure back to England. Drake was among the most successful.

In 1577, he took five ships to America to plunder the Spanish colonies and look for the Northwest Passage. He went all the way around South America and into the Pacific Ocean. The Spanish colonies on the Pacific side were easy to attack because they never expected an English ship to come there! He only had one ship left, the *Golden Hind*, and he filled it with Spanish gold.

Drake explored up the Pacific coast of the Americas, going all the way up to what we know today as Canada. He landed near San Francisco and claimed it for England. Afraid of facing the Spanish to the south, he sailed west across the Pacific. He traded for spices in Asia and returned to England around Africa having sailed around the world!

The king of Spain was furious. He demanded that Elizabeth, the queen of England, punish Drake as a pirate. Instead, she went on board his ship and rewarded him.

Hudson. After working for the Netherlands, Hudson returned to America in 1610 working for England. This time, he sailed further north looking again for the Northwest Passage. He sailed south of Baffin Island in Canada and into one of the world's largest bays. It was named Hudson Bay in his honor.

He sailed around it until winter, trying to find a way to the Pacific Ocean. After suffering through the cold Canadian winter, his men refused to go on in the spring. The men forced Hudson and a few others to stay behind in a small boat. The ship returned to England and nothing more is known about what happened to Henry Hudson.

Hudson's explorations gave England a claim to the land north of New France in Canada. They would eventually establish trading posts there. The English also began to colonize the east coast of North America around the French and Dutch lands.

The Lost Colony. Almost a hundred years after Columbus' first voyage, the English tried to set up a colony in America. Sir Walter Raleigh sponsored a colony on Roanoke Island, North Carolina, in an area they named "Virginia." The colony was founded in 1587. The ships that were to bring it supplies were delayed for three years because of war in Europe. When they arrived in 1590, the colonists were all gone. The settlement was not destroyed, the people were just not there! No one ever found out what happened to them. The Lost Colony is an American history mystery.

Name the place or person.

1.35 _____ English sea dog who sailed around the world attacking Spanish cities and ships

1.36 _____ City built by the Dutch on Manhattan Island

1.37 _____ Explorer working for the Dutch and the English who found a river in New York and a bay in Canada

1.38 _____ Island is where the Lost Colony was founded

1.39 _____ English explorer who found the Grand Banks in 1497

1.40 _____ Name for New Netherlands after it became English

1.41 _____ The Dutch paid about $24 for this important island

1.42 _____ Company that colonized New Netherlands

Review the material in this section to prepare for the Self Test. The Self Test will check your understanding of this section. Any items you miss on this test will show you what areas you will need to restudy in order to prepare for the unit test.

Review Clues

✓ Know the explorers and what they did.

✓ Know what the different nations did in the exploration of the world and America.

✓ Know which nation claimed each part of America.

✓ Know what the explorers were searching for.

SELF TEST 1

Complete this puzzle using the last names of the explorers. Do not leave spaces in the names (each answer, 4 points).

1.01

ACROSS

2. Founder of Quebec, explored Upstate New York, the west end of the St. Lawrence, Lakes Ontario and Huron, "Father of New France," Samuel de _____
4. Sailed for the Dutch and the English, explored the main river of New York and the largest bay in Canada, Henry _____
6. Explored the Mississippi River with Jacques Marquette, Louis _____
7. Explored and named Florida looking for the Fountain of Youth, Ponce de _____
8. English sea dog who sailed around the world robbing the Spanish, Sir Francis _____
9. Sailed for England in 1497 and found the Grand Banks, John _____
10. Spanish conquistador, explored the land between the Mississippi River and Florida, Hernando _____

DOWN

1. Sailed for Spain, led the first voyage around the world, Ferdinand _____
2. Spanish conquistador, explored Texas, Arizona, and New Mexico looking for seven cities of gold, Francisco _____
3. Explored and named the St. Lawrence River as far as Montreal, Jacques _____
5. Discovered the New World sailing for Spain in 1492 while trying to sail to Asia, Christopher _____

Complete these sentences (each answer, 3 points).

1.02   The first European to reach America was the Viking _____ .

1.03   Europeans wanted an all water route to Asia so they could trade for

_____ .

1.04   _____ the Navigator founded a school of navigation in Portugal

and began exploring along the coast of Africa.

1.05   The three ships on Columbus' first voyage in the year _____ were the

Niña, the _____ and the _____ .

1.06   The first European settlement in the United States was the city of

_____ in Florida, founded by the nation of _____ .

1.07   European explorers searched for years for a passage around or through America

called the _____ Passage.

1.08   New France became profitable from trade in _____ .

1.09   The English "Lost Colony" was located on _____ Island in North

Carolina.

1.010   The business that settled the New Netherlands was the Dutch _____

Company.

1.011   New Netherlands was renamed _____ by the British.

1.012   The very first people in America came across the Bering Sea from

_____ long before the Europeans began to explore the world.

1.013   The first nation to find an all water route to Asia was _____ .

Answer true or false (each answer, 1 point).

1.014 _____ Because of the discoveries of Christopher Columbus, Europe found out about America and began to colonize it.

1.015 _____ Magellan was the captain of one of the two ships that safely made it all the way around the world.

1.016 _____ The French claimed all the land drained by the Mississippi River, all of what is now the central part of the United States.

1.017 _____ King Henry and Queen Elizabeth of France sponsored Christopher Columbus' voyages.

1.018 _____ Spain was the first European country to start a successful colony in North America.

1.019 _____ New France held a great deal of land with very few people along the St. Lawrence River, the Great Lakes and the Mississippi River.

1.020 _____ The Dutch paid about $24 in trade goods for Manhattan Island.

Teacher check:

Score _____

Initials _____

Date _____

77 / 96

2. ENGLISH COLONIES

This section of the LIFEPAC will teach about what we call "the original thirteen colonies." These were the thirteen English colonies that joined together to make the United States of America. These thirteen colonies began at different times, and were founded by different people for different purposes.

Each of the colonies had its own government. There was no government for all of the colonies in America. The only government they had together was the English government far across the Atlantic Ocean. Each colony thought of itself as if it were its own little country.

The colonists (people who lived in the colonies) who came over from Europe had to start with nothing in America. They had to build homes, farms, cities, ports, roads, and churches. They also started over with their governments. They set up governments that represented the people, not just the wealthy and the king, like the governments in Europe. All the colonies had a *representative assembly*, a meeting of men elected by the people to make the laws (like Congress today). The colonists liked making their own laws and doing what they wanted with their lives. They liked their independence.

Objectives

Review these objectives. When you have completed this section, you should be able to:

2. Name the nations that claimed land in America and what they claimed.
3. Describe how each of the British colonies were founded and by whom.
4. Describe what the British colonies were like before the Revolution.

Vocabulary

Study these new words. Learning the meanings of these words is a good study habit and will improve your understanding of this LIFEPAC.

acres (ā′ kər). A unit used to measure area, especially the size of land for farming; it is equal to 160 square rods. There are 640 acres in a square mile.

community (kə myü′ nə tē). A group of people living together or sharing common interests.

governor (guv′ ər nər). An official appointed or elected to rule a province or colony.

independence (in′ di pen′ dəns). A freedom from the control, support, influence, or help of others.

refuge (ref′ yüj). Shelter or protection from danger or trouble.

Pronunciation Key: hat, āge, cãre, fär; let, ēqual, tėrm; it, īce; hot, ōpen, ôrder; oil; out; cup, pu̇t, rüle; child; long; thin; /ŦH/ for then; /zh/ for measure; /u/ or /ə/ represents /a/ in about, /e/ in taken, /i/ in pencil, /o/ in lemon, and /u/ in circus.

The First Colonies

Jamestown. The first English colony in America was the city of Jamestown, Virginia. The first settlers were sent by a business called "The Virginia Company of London." The Virginia Company hoped to make lots of money by finding gold or the Northwest Passage. The king gave the company a *charter*, a piece of paper giving them the land of Virginia and the right to rule it in the king's name.

| Jamestown

The company promised the men who went to live in the colony the same rights under the law that they would have in England. England's laws were some of the best in Europe for being fair and giving people freedom. The American colonists would build on this start to make their governments even more fair and free. One hundred men agreed to go to Virginia and work for the company there. These men mostly wanted to get rich quickly and return to England. Nobody realized how much hard work and suffering would be needed to start a colony in the wilderness.

The first ship arrived in Virginia in 1607. The men chose a peninsula on the James River as the place they would build. They named the town and the river after their The First Colonies ruler, King James I. The men quickly built a fort and then spread out to search for gold. Few of them worked to build houses or plant seeds to grow food to eat. Hunger and disease hit hard as a result. Within one year sixty of the one hundred men had died!

The next year (1608) Captain John Smith came to Jamestown with 200 new colonists. Smith forced the men to work planting crops. Those who did not work were kicked out of the colony to starve. This harsh discipline saved the colony. They began to grow food. They also received help from the local Indians who traded food for metal pots, knives, guns, and cloth that they did not have. Sometimes the colonists stole food from the Indians.

More colonists (about 400) came in 1609, but the company had sent too many. The little town could not feed all of them. The winter of 1609-1610 was called the "starving time." In the spring of 1610, only 60 people were still alive. The colony continued in spite of that! More colonists continued to come and they learned from the mistakes of the earlier settlers.

You may have heard of Pocahontas, the daughter of Powhatan, a chief of the Algonquin Indians of Virginia. You may even have seen a cartoon movie about her. The movie is fiction (made up), but she was a real woman. She and her father helped the settlers in Jamestown to survive. In 1613, she became a Christian, changed her named to Rebecca and married John Rolfe, one of the Jamestown colonists. She went to England with him and died there in 1617. Her son, Thomas Rolfe, returned to Virginia after being educated in England.

| Pocahontas statue in Jamestown

John Rolfe also helped Jamestown to survive. He took the tobacco grown by the Indians and by 1616 found a way to remove much of its bitter taste. He sent the new product to Europe where it quickly became very popular. Suddenly, Jamestown had a valuable crop to sell! Tobacco even became the money of the colony.

Some people could not afford the price of passage to America, but they still wanted to come. Many of these people came as *indentured servants*. They would agree to work for someone for 4-7 years in exchange for a ticket to America. After they had served their working time, they were free to get their own land and many became important people in the colony.

Changes helped the colony to grow. In 1618 the Virginia Company promised every individual who came to settle in Virginia 50 **acres** of land. It was called the "head right system." It encouraged families to settle in the new world. The larger the family was the more land it could own. Since land was hard to get in Europe, this attracted many settlers.

The year 1619 was important in Virginia for three reasons. First, the Company allowed the colonists to form the House of Burgesses, the first representative assembly in America. Also, that same year, the Company sent over a boatload of women to become wives of the colonists. This made the colony more permanent as children were born and grew up in Virginia. Thirdly, a *sad* thing happened in 1619. The first African slaves were sold in Virginia. This began over 200 years of slavery in America. This was the first of the original thirteen colonies to be established and to grow successfully.

Name the item or person.

2.1 _____ Married Pocahontas, found a way to make tobacco less bitter

2.2 _____ A piece of paper from the king giving land and the right to rule

2.3 _____ Year that Jamestown was founded

2.4 _____ Algonquin woman who helped the men of Jamestown to survive and married one of them

2.5 _____ People who agreed to work for several years in exchange for passage to America

2.6 _____ Each man who settled in Virginia got 50 acres of land

2.7 _____ The winter of 1609-1610, which only 60 people survived

2.8 _____ The crop that gave Jamestown something to sell

2.9 _____ The company that started Jamestown

2.10 _____ First representative assembly in America

2.11 _____ Two types of people, important to Virginia, who arrived
_____ in 1619

| Pilgrims going to church

Plymouth. Another English colony began in Massachusetts in 1620. It was called Plymouth. It was founded by a group of Christians who landed there by accident. They were supposed to go to Virginia, but they missed and landed in Massachusetts. We call these people the Pilgrims.

The Pilgrims were Christians who were persecuted in England. England had a church run by the government that everyone was supposed to attend. People called *Separatists* wanted to separate from the Anglican (English) Church and worship God in the way they believed was right. The Pilgrims were Separatists who fled to Holland and then, later, to America, intending to settle in Virginia. They took this huge risk so that they could worship God freely in this new land.

They sailed from England in 1620 on board a ship called the *Mayflower*. The ship was very crowded and the trip difficult. Many people were sick by the time the ship accidentally landed in Plymouth Bay, Massachusetts. Because it was November, the colonists needed to build homes before winter began. They decided not to waste more time sailing south, but to settle where they were. Since they were not in Virginia, they had no government for their colony. So, they signed the *Mayflower Compact*, an agreement to form their own government. This was the first of many agreements written in America to establish a government.

The colonists elected a **governor** and began building their colony. As in Virginia, many of the people died of hunger and disease the first winter. An Indian named Squanto, who spoke English and had lost all of his family, came to stay with them. He helped them trade with the Indians in the area. He also showed them what to plant in the spring, where to fish, and how to hunt. The colonists worked hard and had a good harvest in the fall. They invited the nearby Indians, who had become their friends, to come to a three day feast to give thanks to God. This was the first Thanksgiving.

The little colony grew as more of the Pilgrims' Christian brothers and sisters came to join them. They were illegally on the land in the beginning; but by 1621 they were given ownership of it. They never were given a royal charter, which would have made them an independent colony. Plymouth was later joined to the Massachusetts Bay Colony, which did have a charter.

Native Americans. England claimed the land of the original thirteen colonies because Englishmen had explored and colonized it. The English usually ignored the fact that many Native Americans already lived there. The Indians used only part of the land they lived on for farming, leaving the rest as wilderness for hunting. The English took this hunting land, usually without asking permission or paying the Native Americans for it. They saw it only as empty land, free to whoever could claim it. The colonists also thought the Indians were uncivilized and inferior to Europeans. Some of the colonists taught the Indians about Christianity, but only a few tried to protect them and their land.

The Native Americans were pushed out of their land as more and more settlers arrived in America. Sometimes land (called a Reservation) was set aside for their use. The colonists and the Indians sometimes traded peacefully, but often they fought bloody battles with the Indians who usually lost. The Native Americans were frequently treated unfairly by the colonists. They also died in great numbers from European diseases. This would continue for many years, even after the United States was formed.

Answer these questions.

2.12 What do we call the Separatist Christians that settled in Plymouth in 1620?

_____

2.13 What was the name of their ship? _____

2.14 What was the first agreement written in America to make a government?

_____

2.15 Who was the Indian that lived with the colonists and taught them about America?

_____

2.16 Did Plymouth ever get its own charter? _____

2.17 After their first harvest, the colonists had a feast. What was it called?

_____

2.18 Where were the Plymouth colonists supposed to settle? _____

2.19 In your own words, write two sentences about how the colonists usually treated the Native Americans?

_____

_____

_____

New England Colonies

Massachusetts. Some of the people in England did not want to leave the Anglican Church, but to change it. These people were called *Puritans*, because they wanted to purify (make holy) the church. They were also being persecuted. Many of the Puritans were rich and important people, so when they decided to leave England for America, they were better able to prepare than the Pilgrims had been.

| Governor John Winthrop

The Puritans formed a business called the Massachusetts Bay Company in 1629 and got a royal charter for the land surrounding Cape Cod. They organized supplies, settlers and ships. They chose John Winthrop as the colony's first governor. They had sent a few men in advance to start a settlement in 1628, at Salem. When the preparations were made, Winthrop came over in 1630 with hundreds of colonists. They established the city of Boston that same year.

Massachusetts grew very quickly. Boston grew to about 10,000 people in just ten years. Persecution in England and a civil war in the 1640s pushed many Puritans to leave for America. Whole churches would often move to America together.

The Puritans came to America so they could worship in their own way. The churches they set up were not really Anglican. They were *Congregationalist*, churches set up and run by the congregation (people who attended). These people also looked after each other, helped each other with their work, and had a strong sense of **community**. Being part of a Puritan colony meant that you always had people to help you, but it also meant people were always watching you. Puritans thought it was right to check on their neighbors and report their sins to the pastor.

The Puritans also <u>did</u> <u>not</u> allow freedom of religion. Only Puritan men could vote for the colony's government and only Puritan churches were allowed in Massachusetts. Most of the governors and leaders were rich Puritan men who ruled as they thought best. This made many of the colonists unhappy, motivating them to leave and start new colonies all over New England—which became the name for this portion of the northeastern United States.

Connecticut. One of the men who was unhappy in Massachusetts was Thomas Hooker. He was a Puritan pastor who believed that all of the men who lived in the colony should vote, not just the Puritan church members. He and many people who agreed with him moved away from Massachusetts and started the town of Hartford in 1636. Many other people with the same idea started other towns nearby.

In 1639, these people met together to write up a plan of government. The plan they wrote was the *Fundamental Orders of Connecticut*, the first real constitution in American history. A constitution plans out how a government will be organized and run. The *Mayflower Compact* only said that the Pilgrims would establish a government and obey it. It did not explain how the government would work. It was not a real constitution.

Connecticut allowed all free, white men who owned land to vote. The colony did not get a charter until 1662, when one was granted by King Charles II.

Rhode Island. Another pastor who was unhappy in Massachusetts was Roger Williams. Williams argued that not only should everyone be allowed to vote, but that churches that were not Puritan should be permitted. He also said that the King did not own the land, the Indians did! The rulers of Massachusetts were very angry with Williams for saying these things and were going to force him to return to England. Instead, he fled to live with some of the Indians who had become his friends.

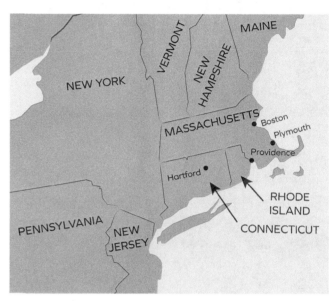

| New England

These same Native Americans sold Williams some land away from Massachusetts where he started the town of Providence in 1636. Again, people who agreed with him came to start more towns nearby. They were able to get a charter from the government in England in 1644.

Rhode Island was a remarkable colony. All of the free, white men could vote. (Most colonies required voters to at least own a certain amount of land or money before they could vote.) It was the very first colony to have real freedom of religion. People could belong to any church they wanted or no church at all. Unlike other colonies, the state (the government) did not control the churches. It also means that the churches had to get their money from their congregations, not the government. In time, this way of keeping the government from controlling the church, often referred to as separation of church and state, became the model for all of the United States.

New Hampshire. The land that is now New Hampshire was given to a man named John Mason by the King of England in 1622. He named it after his home in Hampshire, England. When he did not settle it, people came from Massachusetts to settle there and run the colony's government. Massachusetts ruled the land from 1641 until 1680. That year New Hampshire was given a charter by King Charles II and became an independent colony.

Name the person or thing being described.

2.20 The first real constitution in American history. _____

_____

2.21 People who wanted to purify the Anglican Church and formed the Massachusetts Bay Company to settle in America. _____

2.22 First colony to have real religious freedom. _____

2.23 First governor of Massachusetts Bay. _____

2.24 Man who fled from Massachusetts and founded Rhode Island. _____

_____

2.25 People who were allowed to vote in Massachusetts. _____

_____

2.26 Man who founded Connecticut. _____

2.27 A phrase that describes when government does not control the churches and the churches do not rely on the government for money.

_____

2.28 People who always helped each other and reported each others sins.

_____

2.29 Roger Williams said these people owned the land in America.

_____

Middle Colonies

New York. The Dutch West India Company began to settle families in what is now New York in 1624. To encourage settlers, the company gave large pieces of land to men who brought over settlers to work it. This created a system in New York of rich men who owned the land and poor men who farmed it, paying rent to the owners. The company ran the colony to make a profit and did little to give the people fair government. Thus, New Netherlands, as it was called, grew slowly.

The English did not like having the Dutch in the middle of "their" land. So, in 1664 King Charles II gave a charter for the land of New Netherlands to his brother, James, the Duke of York. The Duke sent a fleet to the colony and the last Dutch governor, Peter Stuyvesant, surrendered without a fight. The colony and its main city were renamed New York.

The *very* selfish Duke of York did not grant his colony more freedom. In fact, he continued to give large pieces of land to his friends to rent to farmers. The colony was not allowed to have a representative assembly until 1683 and even then the people had little power in the government.

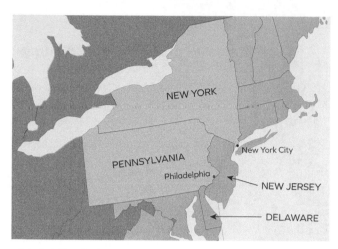

| Middle Colonies

Other nearby colonies had land that could be bought, not just rented. Farmers liked to own their own land. The people also did not like the lack of freedom in New York. New York continued to grow, but much more slowly than the other colonies.

New Jersey. The Duke of York gave the southern part of New Netherlands to two of his friends, Sir George Carteret and Lord John Berkeley, in 1664. They named the land after the English island of Jersey. These men had some experience starting colonies and knew how to attract settlers. They promised freedom of religion and a representative assembly. They sold land at low prices, expecting that they would still collect rents as the colony *proprietors* (the people who owned the colony, almost like having their own kingdom). Colonists liked the freedom and cheap land in New Jersey. The colony grew rapidly.

However, there were many problems. The Duke of York, later King James II, kept trying to control New Jersey even after he gave it away. The colonists also refused to pay rent on the land they had bought. Berkeley finally sold his land in 1674 to some Quakers, a group of Christians who were also persecuted for their beliefs. They made their part of New Jersey into a **refuge** for Quakers. After Carteret died, his share was sold to another group of Quakers in 1680. The colonists still refused to pay rent and the proprietors found they could not make money by owning the colony. So, the colony was turned over to the king in 1702.

Pennsylvania. One of the most famous Quakers was William Penn. He was a very rich man and a friend of the kings of England. Hoping to find a safe place for himself and

| William Penn

HISTORY & GEOGRAPHY 501

LIFEPAC TEST

NAME _____

DATE _____

SCORE _____

HISTORY & GEOGRAPHY 501: LIFEPAC TEST

Match these people (each answer, 2 points).

1. _____ Found a cash crop for Virginia and married Pocahontas

2. _____ Led the first voyage around the world

3. _____ Leader in founding Georgia

4. _____ Explored and named Florida

5. _____ "Father of New France," founded Quebec

6. _____ Founded Maryland as a refuge for Catholics

7. _____ Explored New York for the Dutch and Canada for the British

8. _____ Wrote the Declaration of Independence

9. _____ Found America trying to sail west to Asia

10. _____ Massachusetts pastor, evangelist during the Great Awakening

a. Columbus

b. Jonathan Edwards

c. Thomas Jefferson

d. John Rolfe

e. Ponce de León

f. Magellan

g. Lord Baltimore

h. Champlain

i. Henry Hudson

j. James Oglethorpe

Name the colony (each answer, 3 points).

11. Had complete religious freedom, founded by Roger Williams _____

12. New Netherlands, renamed for the brother of King Charles II _____

13. Northern part of the land given to 8 friends of Charles II, settled by small farmers from Virginia _____

14. Pilgrims came there on the *Mayflower* _____

15. Two colonies founded by William Penn, had wide freedom of religion and fair laws

    a. _____

    b. _____

16. Puritan colony that allowed only men who were Puritan church members to vote, many people left it to start new colonies _____

17. Founded by Thomas Hooker and others who believed everyone, not just Puritans should be allowed to vote _____

18. First colony, started the plantation/slave system raising tobacco _____

19. Southern part of a colony founded by eight friends of Charles II, had a good harbor, West Indies settlers brought slaves _____

Name the item or event (each answer, 3 points).

20. People who worked for someone else for several years to pay for passage to America
_____

21. The very first people to come to North America _____

22. War that gave Britain control of much of North America and the American Revolution began after it _____

23. Laws that closed Boston harbor in response to the Boston Tea Party
_____

24. The first nation to colonize America successfully_____

25. The first British law to tax the colonists, failed _____

26. Name of the route around or through America to Asia
_____

27. The third part of a colonial government besides the council and the governor
_____

28. The men of New France wanted to trade for these _____

29. Paper needed by a person or company to found a colony in America
_____

Choose the correct answer (each answer, 2 points).

30. The _____ forbade the colonists to settle west of the Appalachians.
    a. Proclamation of 1763   b. Quartering Act
    c. Declaratory Act   d. Control Laws

31. All of these were persecuted in England *except* _____ .
    a. Quakers   b. Anglicans
    c. Puritans   d. Catholics

32. The first agreement to make a government in America was the _____ .
a. *Fundamental Orders of Connecticut*   b. Declaration of Independence
c. *Mayflower Compact*   d. Massachusetts Charter

33. The Ottawa Chief who organized a war to drive the colonists out of the land west of the Appalachians was _____ .
a. Squanto   b. Pontiac   c. Coronado   d. Roanoke

34. The first European to reach America was _____ .
a. Columbus   b. Francis Drake   c. Leif Ericson   d. John Cabot

35. The owner of a colony given to him by the king was called a _____ .
a. governor   b. proprietor   c. elder   d. founder

36. The reason the British government began to try to raise taxes in the colonies after 1763 was _____ .
a. it was in debt   b. another war started
c. the king died   d. the colonies revolted

37. The Revolutionary War began at _____ .
a. Concord   b. Jamestown   c. Bunker Hill   d. Lexington

38. The United States was born on the day _____ .
a. Congress voted for independence
b. the Revolutionary War began
c. the Declaration of Independence was accepted
d. Britain granted the colonies independence

39. New France was around _____ .
a. the Gulf of Mexico and the Missouri River
b. the St. Lawrence, Great Lakes and Mississippi River
c. Hudson Bay and the Baffin Island
d. Lake Champlain and the Ottawa River

other Quakers he decided to start a colony in America. He was given a huge piece of land by Charles II in 1681 to pay off a debt the king owed him. The land was named Pennsylvania (Penn's woods).

Penn set out to create a colony that was as free as possible in both religion and government. He was very fair toward the Native Americans, paying them for the land before he sold to settlers. He set up his colony with freedom of religion for all Christians except Catholics (who were hated in England), no government church, a representative assembly, a fair constitution, and cheap land.

The colony grew very quickly. Penn himself planned the capital, Philadelphia (The City of Brotherly Love) on the Delaware River. It soon became an important port and the largest city in the colonies. Penn's family were the proprietors of the colony until the Americans rebelled against England in 1776.

Delaware. The Duke of York gave the land of Delaware to William Penn in 1682 so that his colony would have an outlet to the sea. It was considered part of Pennsylvania at first, and had the same freedoms as that colony. The colonists in Delaware eventually wanted to have their own assembly, separate from Pennsylvania. Their request was granted in 1704. The colony was under the governor of Pennsylvania and owned by the Penn family until 1776.

| Delaware gave Penn's lands access to the Atlantic Ocean.

Match these items. One will be used more than once.

2.30	_____ The two men who founded New Jersey _____	a. William Penn
		b. proprietor
2.31	_____ Sent a fleet to conquer New Netherlands	c. George Carteret
2.32	_____ Colony given to William Penn by the Duke of York	d. John Berkeley
		e. New York
2.33	_____ Colony given to William Penn by Charles II to pay a debt	f. Duke of York
		g. New Jersey
2.34	_____ Rich Quaker, friend of the English kings	h. Delaware
2.35	_____ Had been named New Netherlands by the Dutch	i. Pennsylvania
2.36	_____ Farmers had to rent from rich landowners, colony that grew slowly	
2.37	_____ Colony founded by two friends of the Duke of York, was sold to the Quakers and then given to the king	
2.38	_____ The owner of a colony	
2.39	_____ Man who was fair to the Indians, paying them for the land	
2.40	_____ Wanted a colony that was as free as possible in religion and government	

Southern Colonies

| The Southern Colonies

Virginia. Virginia was the very first English colony in America, begun at Jamestown in 1607. The Virginia Company ran the colony until 1624. That year King James I took away the Company's charter and brought Virginia under royal control.

Virginia grew and expanded west, pushed by the demand for tobacco. However, tobacco requires a large amount of hand labor. Many of the colonists found they could raise it better on plantations than on small farms. At first, the workers on the plantations were indentured servants; but once they were free, these people went off to get their own land. Free people in America did not want to work for someone else. So, the plantation owners started buying black slaves (people who were captured in Africa) to do their work. The slaves were considered to be property and had no rights and no protection under the law.

This plantation system spread all over the south. Most of the southern states had large landowners who raised a cash crop for sale using slaves. These men often became very rich and thought of themselves as better than those who worked the land for them. They were often well educated. Many of the Founding Fathers, the men who fought for American freedom and served in its first governments, were plantation owners from Virginia.

Maryland. Maryland was founded by a man named George Calvert, whose title was Lord Baltimore. He was Catholic, which meant he had been persecuted in England, too. King Charles I gave him a charter for the land just north of Virginia in 1632. Baltimore named it after the king's wife, Henrietta Maria. George Calvert died just before the colony's charter was signed and his son Celcilius (who became the new Lord Baltimore) began the colony in 1634.

The Calverts wanted a colony that could be a refuge for Catholics, but they also wanted to make money by land sales and rents. That meant they would have to attract colonists who were not Catholic. The colony was allowed to have an assembly to encourage settlers. In 1649, Lord Baltimore asked the assembly to pass the Toleration Act. It gave freedom of religion to all Christians, including Catholics. It was the law in Maryland for many years.

Maryland grew quickly. People liked the freedom of religion there and the Calverts ruled the colony fairly most of the time. Also, they learned from Virginia and had a cash crop, tobacco, from the start. Much of the land was filled with plantations as in Virginia. Most of the colonists, however, were Protestants who did not like being ruled by a Catholic.

The civil war in England and religious hatred caused problems for the Calvert family. The colony was taken away from them in the 1690s and became a royal colony; but in 1715 it was given back to the Calverts, because the newest Lord Baltimore was in the Anglican Church. The new proprietors ended the freedom of religion for Catholics in 1718. The Calverts were proprietors of Maryland until 1776.

North Carolina. King Charles II gave the land named Carolina to eight of his friends, some of the richest and most powerful men in England, in 1663. The colony's first government was created by the Fundamental Constitutions, written by one of the proprietors in 1669. The colonists were unhappy with the constitutions and in 1693 it was changed to give the assembly more power.

| Cotton was grown in colonial North Carolina.

The northern part of Carolina was settled by farmers from Virginia. These were hard working men who were unhappy that rich plantation owners controlled the government in Virginia. The coast of what would be North Carolina did not have any good harbors. This made it difficult to ship out the cash crops from plantations. All these factors caused what would become North Carolina to be the one southern state that was not principally plantations. It was a colony of small farmers.

Northern Carolina was so different from the southern part that the two were given different governors in about 1710. Shortly after that the proprietors sold the colony back to the king, because they were having trouble protecting it against the Spanish to the south. North and South Carolina became separate royal colonies in 1729.

South Carolina. Southern Carolina had the best harbor in the south. In 1680, a city named Charleston, after King Charles, was founded there. The great harbor and warm weather attracted many rich men from the West Indies who settled in South Carolina. They brought their slaves and used them to build plantations to raise indigo (to make blue dye) and rice. These crops could be sold to other countries for a good profit using the harbor at Charleston. South Carolina became a plantation state with a large population of slaves. The people of the state would later be among the strongest defenders of slavery in America.

Georgia. Georgia was the last of the original thirteen colonies to be established. King George II gave a charter for the land to a group of kind hearted men led by James Oglethorpe in 1732. These men wanted to start a colony to help people in debt. People who could not pay their debts in the 1700s were usually put into prison. Oglethorpe and his group hoped the debtors could go to America instead, farm the land there, and pay off their debts.

The first colonists came in 1733 with Oglethorpe as the first governor. The colony had trouble from the start. The board of directors, the men who were given the charter, set up strict laws for the colony. The colonists did not like the laws which prevented them from having large plantations and slaves to work them. They also did not have an assembly. Moreover, England went to war with Spain around 1740. Oglethorpe tried to capture Florida during the war and had to defend Georgia from Spanish attacks.

| Peaches are grown in Georgia.

The proprietors were supposed to return the colony to the king in 1754. They gave it up two years early because of the problems of defending it and complaints from the colonists about the laws. The king gave the colony a representative assembly and removed the strict laws. Georgia became a plantation/slave colony, like most of the south, growing rice and indigo. It did not have many people in it by 1776 because it started so late and had so many problems.

Complete these sentences.

2.41 Almost all of the southern colonies raised cash crops on _____ worked by African _____ .

2.42 The one southern colony that was made up of mainly small farms was _____ .

2.43 The founder of Maryland was Lord _____ .

2.44 Georgia was founded by a group of kind hearted men led by_____ _____ who wanted to help people who were in _____ .

2.45   Maryland was founded as a refuge for _____ .

2.46   The first English colony in America was _____ .

2.47   _____ was the last of the original thirteen colonies.

2.48   The _____ Act gave all the Christian colonists in

Maryland freedom of religion.

2.49   _____ was the colony that had a good harbor at

Charleston and attracted rich settlers from the West Indies who brought their slaves

along.

2.50   The main crop of Maryland and Virginia was _____ .

2.51   The main crops of South Carolina and Georgia were rice and _____ .

Review the material in this section to prepare for the Self Test. The Self Test will check your understanding of this section and the previous section. Any items you miss on this test will show you what areas you will need to restudy in order to prepare for the unit test.

Review Clues

   ✓   Know how and by whom each colony was founded.

   ✓   Know the story and names of the important people in the colonies.

   ✓   Know the names of the new ideas in italics.

SELF TEST 2

Name the colony (each answer, 3 points).

2.01   A <u>town</u> that was the very first English colony in America, founded in 1607 by the Virginia Company of London _____

2.02   Founded as a refuge for Catholics, the Toleration Act gave freedom of religion to all Christians _____

2.03   Founded by Puritans, only Puritans were allowed to vote, many people left this colony to start new ones _____

2.04   First of the original thirteen colonies, began the plantation/slave system in the south raising tobacco _____

2.05   Founded by Thomas Hooker who wanted a colony where all the men, not just those in the Puritan church could vote _____

2.06   Last colony founded, started to help people in debt _____

2.07   Colony began when the *Mayflower* landed in Massachusetts by mistake, the first Thanksgiving was there _____

2.08   Founded by Roger Williams, first colony to have complete freedom of religion

_____

2.09   New Netherlands, built by the Dutch West India Co., taken by the Duke of York, grew slowly due to lack of freedom and land to buy _____

2.010   Founded by two friends of the Duke of York who gave them the land, eventually it was sold to the Quakers _____

2.011   Founded by eight wealthy friends of King Charles II, had a great harbor at Charleston, settlers from the West Indies brought in their slaves to grow indigo and rice _____

2.012   Founded by William Penn with freedom of religion and good laws, Philadelphia was its capital and America's largest city _____

2.013   Given to William Penn by the Duke of York to give his colony an outlet to the sea, became a separate colony _____

2.014   Given to John Mason, but the people of Massachusetts settled it and ruled it until it became a separate colony _____

2.015   Southern colony that did not have a good port, settled by farmers from Virginia, made up mainly of small farms _____

Match the following people (each answer, 2 points).

2.016   _____ Saved Jamestown by forcing the men to work

2.017   _____ Ran away from Massachusetts, paid the Native Americans for land to start a colony

2.018   _____ Catholic who founded Maryland

2.019   _____ Led the group that founded Georgia

2.020   _____ Quaker who was given land in America by the king of England to pay off a debt

2.021   _____ Gave Virginia a money-making crop and married Pocahontas

2.022   _____ Native American who helped the Plymouth colonists

2.023   _____ Discovered America trying to sail west to Asia from Europe on the *Niña*, the *Pinta*, and the *Santa Maria*

2.024   _____ First governor of Massachusetts

2.025   _____ Explored Texas, Arizona, and New Mexico looking for seven cities of gold

a.   Columbus

b.   John Smith

c.   Lord Baltimore

d.   James Oglethorpe

e.   Coronado

f.   Roger Williams

g.   William Penn

h.   John Rolfe

i.   Squanto

j.   John Winthrop

Complete the sentences using words from the list (each answer, 2 points).

Mayflower Compact	Fundamental Orders of Connecticut	charter
Puritans	indentured servants	Pilgrims
spices	Northwest Passage	proprietor
	representative assembly	

2.026 To start a colony a person or company needed a _____ from the king that gave them the land and the right to rule it.

2.027 The _____ was the first real constitution in America.

2.028 By 1776 all of the colonies had a _____ , a meeting of men, elected by the people to make the laws.

2.029 The person who owned a colony given them by the king was called the _____ .

2.030 Europeans wanted a water route to Asia so they could buy _____ .

2.031 The _____ was the first agreement to make a government in America.

2.032 The _____ were persecuted in England, but were rich enough to make careful preparations and get a charter to go to America.

2.033 The _____ were Separatists who fled England and then went to America so they could worship God as they wanted.

2.034 Many of the explorers of America were looking for the _____ _____ through it so they could reach Asia.

2.035 _____ were people who were able to get passage to America by promising to work for someone for several years.

Answer true or false (each answer, 1 point).

2.036 _____ Many of the first settlers at Jamestown and Plymouth died.

2.037 _____ The "head right system" gave every individual in Virginia about $20 worth of gold.

2.038 _____ The Native American people were treated unfairly by most of the English colonists who took their land without paying.

2.039 _____ England had a church run by the government called the Anglican Church.

2.040 _____ Catholics and Quakers were persecuted in England.

2.041 _____ The first colonists in Georgia liked the strict laws of the colony.

2.042 _____ New France was built around the St. Lawrence River, the Great Lakes, and the Mississippi River.

2.043 _____ The Portuguese explorer Prince Henry was the first European ever to reach America.

2.044 _____ Many of the colonies were given or sold back to the King of England.

2.045 _____ Ponce de León explored and named Florida looking for the fountain of youth.

Teacher check:

Score _____

Initials _____

Date _____

76 / 95

3. REVOLUTION BEGINS

A revolt is refusing to obey someone in authority or fighting against them. You can revolt against parents, bosses, or governments. In 1776 the American colonies revolted against the British government (England changed its name to Great Britain in 1707). This revolt is called the *American Revolution.* The Americans revolted by refusing to pay taxes, boycotting British goods, fighting a war, and setting up a republic.

The war is called the *War for Independence* or the *Revolutionary War.* Many people also call the war just "the Revolution," but the Revolution involved much more than just the war. The Revolution was <u>everything</u> that happened to change the British colonies in America to the United States of America, a republic.

This section will explain what the British colonies were like before the Revolution. It will look at why the colonists became unhappy with the British government and why they decided to revolt. Even after they revolted, they might have stayed a part of Great Britain with more freedom. However, they decided instead to fight for independence. They wrote the Declaration of Independence to explain their reasons. The day that declaration was accepted is the day we say the United States was born, July 4, 1776.

Objectives

Review these objectives. When you have completed this section, you should be able to:

2. Name the nations that claimed land in America and what they claimed.
4. Describe what the British colonies were like before the Revolution.
5. Describe the French and Indian War and why it changed Britain's thinking about its American colonies.
6. Describe the conflicts with Britain that led the Americans to revolt.
7. Describe the beginning of the Revolutionary War and the birth of the United States of America.

Vocabulary

Study these new words. Learning the meanings of these words is a good study habit and will improve your understanding of this LIFEPAC.

ambush (am' bu̇ sh). A surprise attack on an approaching enemy from a hiding place.

boycott (boi' kot). To join together against and agree not to buy from, sell to, or associate with a person, business, or nation.

evangelist (i van' jə l əst). A person who preaches the gospel to win people to Christ.

frontier (frun tir'). The last edge of settled country, where the wild countryside begins.

jury (ju̇ r ē). A group of citizens chosen to hear evidence in a case brought before a court of law; it, not the judge, decides the case based on the evidence.

militia (mə lish' ə). An army of citizens who are not regular soldiers but who are trained for war or any other emergency.

monopoly (mə nop' ə lē). The complete control of a product or service.

petition (pə tish' ən). A written request to someone in authority for some right or privilege often signed by many people.

republic (ri pub' lik). A government in which the citizens elect representatives to manage the government which is usually headed by a president.

Pronunciation Key: hat, āge, cãre, fär; let, ēqual, tėrm; it, īce; hot, ōpen, ôrder; oil; out; cup, pu̇t, rüle; child; long; thin; /ŦH/ for then; /zh/ for measure; /u/ or /ə/ represents /a/ in about, /e/ in taken, /i/ in pencil, /o/ in lemon, and /u/ in circus.

America Before the Revolution

America, place of freedom. The American colonists at first thought of themselves as Englishmen living away from home. However, as the years passed, their children and grandchildren began to think differently. They did not remember Great Britain. America was their home.

America was a very free place compared to Europe. In Britain, the very rich noblemen who had titles like Lords, Dukes, and Earls owned most of the land and controlled the government. They did not work but they held all the power. Everyone was expected to obey them and they controlled the lives of the people who lived on their land. With very few exceptions, the only way to become a noble was to be born as one. So, people who were hard working and smart could never become powerful, while nobles who might be lazy and stupid were powerful anyway.

In America, however, almost anyone could own land and very few nobles ever came to the colonies to live. As a result, the people who became rich by their own hard work often became powerful. The government was usually controlled by the rich, but even the poorest farmer who owned a little bit of land could vote. That meant he had some say in the government. This made Americans much more free and independent than the people of Britain.

Trade. Britain had many laws to control trade with the American colonies. But, some of the laws were very silly. For example, if an American wanted to sell some rice to a French island in the West Indies, the ship was supposed to travel all the way across the Atlantic Ocean to Britain first! Then, the rice would be taxed and sent back across the Atlantic to the French island. Also, certain important products like tobacco and supplies for the navy could only be sold to Britain, even if Britain could not buy all that the Americans could grow! The idea behind these laws was that the colonies would trade only with Britain, making more money for Britain and its people.

| Some colonists worked as shoemakers

The colonists knew these laws were silly and usually ignored them. They would sell their crops directly to the French islands in the West Indies and anywhere else they wanted. The British government made the laws, but for many years before 1763, it did not enforce them. Britain was busy fighting wars in Europe and dealing with other problems. It left the colonies and their governments alone to do as they wanted. Thus, Americans became used to trading freely and running their own affairs.

Government. All of the original thirteen colonies had similar kinds of governments. Most colonies had a governor, a council, and an assembly. The governor ran the government most of the time and held most of the power. He made sure the taxes were collected, salaries were paid, roads were repaired, and the **militia** was available to protect the colonist from the Indian attacks. In a few of the colonies, the colonists voted for a governor. In the other colonies, the king or the proprietor chose the governor.

The council was a group of important men in the colony who helped the governor. They were chosen by the governor. They had to approve any laws passed by the assembly. In some colonies, they could write laws for the assembly to consider. They also were the most important court in the colony.

The assembly was the voice of the people in the colony. In almost all of the colonies, men who owned land or a certain amount of money could vote. They voted for the people who would be part of the assembly. They chose men they thought would do the things they wanted done.

The assembly was very important in the colonial government. It had to approve all of the taxes. This meant that even a powerful governor, appointed by the king, had to listen to what the assembly wanted. If he did not, the assembly might not give him the money he needed to run the government or even to pay his own salary! Thus, in America, colonists were able to vote for representatives who had some real power in the government. Americans had a lot of freedom both in their trade and in their government.

The Great Awakening. The Great Awakening was the name of an large *revival* that took place in the 1730s and 40s in America. A revival is a time when many people accept Jesus Christ as their Lord and Savior. This revival saw thousands of people in America either become Christians or decide to live as better Christians. It spread all over the colonies.

| George Whitefield preaching to crowd

Two men were important **evangelists** in this revival. One was Jonathan Edwards, a pastor from Massachusetts. Another was George Whitefield, a pastor from Britain. Edwards spoke mainly in his own church, but his sermons and writings were printed all over the colonies. George Whitefield was a great speaker who traveled all over the American colonies preaching the Word of God. These men convinced many people that they needed Jesus in their lives.

The Great Awakening may have been God's way of getting America ready for the Revolution. He knew the Americans were about to start a new nation, even if they did not realize it. Because of the Great Awakening, many of the men who would fight for American freedom, decide for American independence, and write American constitutions would be men of God.

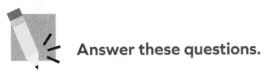

Answer these questions.

3.1   What were the three parts of most of the colonial governments?

a. _____

b. _____

c. _____

3.2   Why were the assemblies able to control the governors?

_____

_____

3.3   Why didn't the nobles rule America?

_____

3.4   Usually, who could vote in the colonies?

_____

_____

3.5   What was the Great Awakening? _____

3.6   Who were the two evangelists of the Great Awakening?

a. _____   b. _____

3.7   What was the name for all of the things that changed the British colonies into the

United States of America? _____

3.8   What did most Americans do about Britains trade laws?

_____

3.9   Did Britain enforce its trade laws and control the colonial governments before 1763?

_____

3.10   What was the purpose of the British trade laws?

_____

_____

3.11   Who chose the men who would be part of the assembly?

_____

Indian Wars. The Native Americans tried to stop the British colonists from taking their land; but they did not organize armies to fight like the Europeans did. The Indians often would sneak up on a settlement and attack the colonists without warning, killing everyone, including the women and children. These were called *massacres*. Sometimes the colonists would respond with massacres of their own. Sometimes several of the Indian tribes would work together, attacking many settlements at the same time. These attacks made the American **frontier** a very dangerous place.

Americans on the frontier learned to be prepared for the danger of Indian attacks. Most American men learned to shoot a gun early in their life and always owned one. They would form militia groups to fight the Indians and punish them for attacking settlers. Thus, the colonies had an army. It was an army of farmers, shopkeepers, pastors, and school teachers who could quickly take their guns, join the militia, and fight an enemy. This was the army that would fight for independence.

New France. France claimed all of the land in the center part of the United States. The British colonies ended at the Appalachian Mountains. The Americans did not like this. They wanted to expand westward into the rich land on the French side of the mountains. The Americans often would settle there anyway. Britain and France were enemies at this time. Battles often occurred between the British and French colonists.

New France still had very few colonists. The British colonists outnumbered them by a large margin. However, the French were well organized for fighting and they only had one government. The British colonies had thirteen. The French also had many Indian allies. The Native Americans knew the French wanted to trade for furs, not take land for farms, so they often would fight with the French against the British.

| Thirteen original colonies

Britain and France went to war several times from 1680 to 1763. When a war started in Europe, the colonists in America would also fight each other. The British government let the colonial militias do the fighting in America for most of that time. When the war ended in Europe, the two sides would sign a treaty that might give one side some of the other's land in America. Very little changed until the last war fought between the French and the British in America. It was called the French and Indian War.

French and Indian War. The French and Indian War began in America in 1754. A Virginia militia officer named George Washington tried to capture Fort Duquesne, which the French had built in the Ohio River Valley, a rich farmland both sides wanted. The French, with their Indian friends, attacked Washington who had built an emergency fort called Fort Necessity. Washington was forced to surrender and was allowed to take his men home.

For the first time, the British government sent over its army to fight in America. George Washington worked as an aide (military assistant) for the British commander, General Edward Braddock. Washington and the other colonists tried to warn Braddock about how the French in America fought by **ambushes**, using Indian allies. Braddock would not listen. He tried to fight the war his way.

He took his army to attack Fort Duquesne marching in the open and building a road as they went. The men wore bright red uniforms and did not watch for ambushes. He expected the French army to march out to meet him in the open. Instead, the French attacked, without warning, from behind the trees while the army was marching by.

The British were defeated that day. General Braddock was killed in the battle. George Washington had two of the horses he was riding killed and several bullets went through his coat. But, God protected him from harm. The badly beaten British army retreated.

The French had several more victories in America before the British turned things around. A new British leader in *Parliament* (the British Congress) began to organize the army for victory. His name was William Pitt. He chose clever generals who fought well. He made sure they had the supplies they needed. Most important of all, he had a strategy for winning the war.

Pitt ordered the generals to work on taking the French forts, especially those on the St. Lawrence River. This was the only way in and out of New France. Once those forts were taken, the French soldiers could not get supplies or new troops. The strategy worked well. Fort Duquesne was captured in 1758. It was renamed Fort Pitt and would one day become the city of Pittsburgh. Several other important forts in New York were taken that year.

The next year the British captured the fortress city of Quebec. Quebec was built high on a cliff above the St. Lawrence River. Ships could not safely travel on the river with the cannons of Quebec firing on them. The British commander General James Wolfe found a way up the cliffs. The French commander, Montcalm, marched out to meet him. Both generals died in the battle, but the British won. The rest of New France was captured without much difficulty.

The British had beaten the French very badly in America. They also won the war in Europe where the two sides were also fighting. So, when the Treaty of Paris was signed in 1763, ending the war, France lost all of its land in America. Britain took all of the French land in Canada and all of the land east of the Mississippi River in the United States. Spain took the French land west of the Mississippi (it was given back to France later).

This war was very important to the colonists for several reasons. The Americans saw that the British could be defeated in battle. The war taught many of the colonial militia men how to fight in a big war. The colonists no longer needed the power of Britain to protect them from the French. The victory also made the British government very proud and it began to make some foolish mistakes handling the colonies. The American Revolution would begin a few years after this war.

Answer true or false.

3.12 _____ The Treaty of London ended the French and Indian War.

3.13 _____ The French and Indian War allowed many of the Americans to gain experience fighting a big war.

3.14 _____ The Native Americans did very little to stop the colonists from taking their land.

3.15 _____ Spain took France's land in Canada while Britain took all of the land around the Mississippi River after the French and Indian War.

3.16 _____ The British colonies had more people than New France.

3.17 _____ Native Americans would help the French against the British because the French did not want land for farms.

3.18 _____ The new leader of the British Parliament who organized the British victory was William Pitt.

3.19 _____ The French ambushed and killed General Braddock.

3.20 _____ The French and Indian War began when George Washington attempted to take Fort Duquesne and then was defeated at Fort Necessity.

3.21 _____ Most American men owned a gun and knew how to use it.

3.22 _____ The American frontier was a very safe place.

3.23 _____ After the French and Indian War the Americans no longer needed protection from the French.

3.24 _____ The militia was the American army.

3.25 _____ George Washington was badly injured when the French attacked General Braddock's army.

3.26 _____ France lost its land in America as a result of the loss of the French and Indian War, a well as its loss of the war being fought in Europe at the same time.

3.27 _____ The French commander at the battle of Quebec was Edward Braddock while the French general was Montcalm.

3.28 _____ William Pitt's strategy was to take the French forts, especially on the St. Lawrence.

3.29 _____ The American Revolution began a few years after the French and Indian War.

Conflicts with Britain

Proclamation of 1763. After the French and Indian War, the Americans and the British government came into more and more conflict. The first happened in 1763. After the French had been defeated, several of the Indians decided to attack the British colonists to stop them from moving across the Appalachian Mountains. These Native Americans were led by a man named Pontiac, an Ottawa chief.

Pontiac convinced many of the tribes all along the frontier to join in the war. They planned to attack and destroy the British forts and then attack the unprotected settlers. They began in early 1763. Many of the forts were taken and hundreds of settlers were killed. Several important forts survived, however, and the militia as well as the British army quickly began to fight back. Pontiac was not able to get help from the French and finally had to make peace.

The sudden attack startled the British government. They had just finished a long war and did not want another one right away with the Indians. So, they decided to keep the settlers away from the Indians by issuing the Proclamation of 1763. The Proclamation ordered the American colonists not to settle west of the Appalachian Mountains unless the Indians gave up the land by treaty.

This made the colonists angry. They had fought the French and Indian War so they could settle that land. They were not going to stop now. They did not care that the Indians owned that land. They ignored the Proclamation and settled across the mountains anyway. That made the British government angry.

Changes in Britain. The war in America and Europe had been very expensive for Great Britain. By 1763, the British government was deeply in debt. Also, the victory had given the British a huge empire in America that they felt needed to be properly controlled. The British also began to think that the colonies should pay taxes to help cover the cost of the war, which was fought for their protection.

The *Prime Minister* (leader of the British Parliament and government), George Grenville, began to change the way Britain treated the colonies after 1763 with the approval of King George III. He began by ordering all of the trade laws, even the foolish ones, to be strictly enforced. He passed the Sugar Act that put very high taxes on sugar and rum, important trade items between America and the West Indies.

| King George III

If someone broke the trade laws, Grenville ordered that they had to stand trial in Admiralty Court. These courts did not use a **jury** and the person on trial was assumed to be guilty. In a normal court, a person is assumed to be innocent and the government must prove he is guilty. This scared Americans who felt their rights as Englishmen were being taken away.

Grenville also passed the Quartering Act. This law forced the colonists to provide food and housing for the British soldiers in America. The colonial governments were not happy about having to suddenly take over this expensive and often difficult job. Many refused to cooperate.

Stamp Act. Finally, Grenville wanted to raise money in the colonies to help pay some of the costs of governing them. Britain had never taxed the colonists before. The only British taxes had been on goods to control trade. The colonists had paid taxes to their colonial government only after the colony's assembly had voted for them; but Grenville changed that with the Stamp Act of 1765.

The Stamp Act required that all important papers, like bills of sale, deeds for land, newspapers, wills, and even playing cards, had to have a stamp sold by the government. The sale of the stamps would raise a lot of money for Britain. Grenville and the Parliament made this law without the approval of the colonial assemblies. Moreover, people who disobeyed the law were to be sent to the Admiralty Court!

The Americans were very angry about the Stamp Act. They cried, "No taxation without representation." The colonial assemblies tried to convince Grenville that the law was wrong. The colonists also began to work together to fight it.

Nine of the thirteen colonies sent representatives to the Stamp Act Congress in 1765. It was their first try to bring about an assembly of all the colonies. The Congress argued that taxes could only be raised by an assembly that represented the people of the land. Since the colonies could not vote for representatives to Parliament, Parliament could not tax the colonies! The British government would not listen.

The Americans found a better way to fight the Stamp Act when they started a boycott of British goods. British merchants became alarmed when Americans quit buying their cloth, tea, cups, and tools. The merchants complained to the British government, which listened to them.

Also, many of the angry colonists began to take the law into their own hands. They formed secret groups like the "Sons of Liberty." These groups beat up or threatened men who agreed to sell the stamps. They also damaged businesses that did not keep the boycott. They frightened people so badly that on the day the stamps were to be sold, <u>no one</u> would sell them!!

A new Prime Minister decided to end the Stamp Act. He realized that the colonists would not pay it and that British merchants were losing money. However, Parliament insisted that it *did* have the power to tax the colonies. It repealed (took back) the Stamp Act, but passed the Declaratory Act at the same time. The Declaratory Act stated that Parliament had the right to control the colonies in any way they wanted.

Name the item or person.

3.30 _____ Prime Minister of Britain who passed the Stamp Act

3.31 _____ Court that had no juries and the accused person was assumed to be guilty

3.32 _____ Law that required the colonists to house and feed British soldiers

3.33 _____ Ordered Americans not to settle west of the Appalachian Mountains

3.34 _____ Law that put high taxes on rum and sugar

3.35 _____ Tax on all important papers

3.36 _____ Secret group that beat up stamp sellers and people who did not keep the boycott

3.37 _____ Parliament said it had the right to do anything it wanted to control the colonies

3.38 _____ Meeting of nine of the thirteen colonies to discuss the Stamp Act, the first assembly for all the colonies

3.39 _____ Ottawa chief that led a Native American attack on the British colonists in 1763

Answer these questions.

3.40 What did the colonists mean when they said, "No taxation without representation?"

_____

3.41 How did the Americans respond to the Proclamation of 1763?

_____

3.42 Why did the British government want to tax the colonists after 1763?

_____

Townshend Acts. Britain still needed money. So, a new set of taxes was set up by Charles Townshend, who was in charge of the British treasury in 1767. The new taxes, named after Townshend, were put on goods shipped from Britain, not directly on the colonists. Things such as paint, lead, glass, paper, and tea were taxed. This was very close to the old taxes to control trade and the British thought the Americans would accept them.

The government also made it easier for officials to search American homes and businesses for illegal trade items. Moreover, it threatened to close the New York assembly because it had not obeyed the Quartering Act. The taxes and the new laws frightened the Americans. They began to believe the British were working to take away their liberty.

The Americans organized another boycott. Many important people in the colonies wrote pamphlets urging people to stand up for their rights. Several began to argue that Parliament had no authority in America, but most people did not agree with that, yet. Eventually, the boycott forced the British to end the Townshend taxes in 1770, except for the one on tea. It was kept just to remind the Americans that Parliament could indeed tax them!

Boston Massacre. Boston was a leading city in the fight against the British. The Sons of Liberty were very strong there. It was also the home of Samuel Adams, a man who led the fight against the British. Extra British troops were sent to Boston to keep order. This only caused further trouble.

Some of these soldiers were on guard duty in March of 1770 when a crowd of unarmed citizens began throwing things at them. The soldiers opened fire and five of the people in the crowd were killed. *Patriots* (people who supported the American side of the fight) called it the Boston Massacre. Stories about it spread all over the colonies, making people even angrier at the British.

| The Boston Massacre

Boston Tea Party. In 1773 another Prime Minister made yet another mistake in handling the colonies. He gave the British East India Company a **monopoly** on the sale of tea to the American colonies. The prices were so cheap that many people saw it as a trick to get them to accept the tax on the tea. Rather than accept the tax, the Sons of Liberty decided to get rid of the tea.

The Sons of Liberty in Boston disguised themselves as Indians and went on board the tea ships in the harbor on December 13, 1773. They took the big crates of tea, broke them open and threw them into the harbor. It was called the Boston Tea Party. They did not hurt anyone. They just refused to accept the tea with the tax on it. Other colonies also refused the tea.

Intolerable Acts. The Boston Tea party was the last straw as far as the British government was concerned. Valuable private property had been destroyed! They passed a series of laws we call the Intolerable Acts. These laws closed Boston harbor, cutting the city off from its main way of making money and its way of bringing in food. The city was occupied by British troops and a British general put in charge of it. The Massachusetts charter was changed so that Britain appointed all of the important officials. Town meetings were forbidden. Massachusetts lost in one swoop many of the rights and freedoms Americans had enjoyed for years.

First Continental Congress. The Americans were deeply shocked by the Intolerable Acts. Most of the colonies sent supplies to Boston. They also agreed to meet together to decide what to do about the Acts. The thirteen separate colonies were beginning to realize they had to work together to defend their rights.

The First Continental Congress met in September of 1774 in Philadelphia. All of the colonies, except Georgia, sent representatives. Many of the men we call the "founding fathers" of the United States were there. George Washington, John Adams, Samuel Adams, and Patrick Henry were all at this meeting.

The Congress passed several agreements. One was another boycott, to last until the Acts were withdrawn. Another stated that Americans had the right to their own assemblies, which were the only ones that could tax them. They also sent a **petition** to the king asking him to protect, not take away, their freedoms. They also agreed to meet again in May of 1775 if their demands were not met.

| The First Continental Congress met in Philadelphia

Most of the men at the First Continental Congress did not want to be independent from Britain. They just wanted their rights as British citizens. They still hoped that Parliament and King George III would understand. They wanted the freedom to run their own governments and businesses the way they had before the French and Indian War. However, they were getting more and more frustrated at how the British were treating them.

Complete these sentences.

3.43   The _____ Acts put taxes on things like paint, lead, glass, and tea coming from Britain.

3.44   Sons of Liberty disguised as _____ threw tea into the harbor at an event named the Boston _____ .

3.45   The First _____ met to decide what to do about the Intolerable Acts.

3.46   The _____ was when British soldiers fired into a crowd killing five people in Boston.

3.47   When the Townshend Acts were ended, the tax on _____ was kept.

3.48   The First Continental Congress started another _____ and agreed to meet again in _____ if their demands were not met.

3.49   Patriots were people who supported the _____ side.

3.50 The _____ Acts closed Boston Harbor, put the city under

military rule, and took away many of the colony's freedoms.

3.51 Most of the men at the First Continental Congress (did / did not) want to be

independent of Britain.

Revolt

Lexington and Concord. The people of Massachusetts began to prepare for war after the Intolerable Acts. They gathered guns and ammunition at different places, including a town called Concord, about 15 miles from Boston. The colony's militia began to drill (practice for war). The Massachusetts assembly was also meeting illegally at Concord and the British wanted its leaders captured.

General Gage was in charge of the British army that was occupying Boston. In April of 1775, he sent 700 soldiers at night to the towns of Lexington and Concord. He wanted to destroy the supplies at those towns and hoped to capture the colonial leaders, but his men were being watched closely by the Sons of Liberty.

The Sons of Liberty knew the British were going to march, they just did not know which way they would go, across land or by sea across the harbor. They arranged for someone to watch and put a signal in the steeple of the Old North Church in Boston. The signal was one lantern if the soldiers were going by land or two if by sea. When the two lamps were put up in the steeple, two men rode hard out of Boston on fast horses to warn the patriots at Lexington and Concord. Paul Revere became the most famous of the two riders because Henry Wadsworth Longfellow wrote a stirring poem about his desperate ride to warn his countrymen.

| Statue of Paul Revere

Revere was stopped at Lexington, but the other rider reached Concord in time.

When the British soldiers reached Lexington they were met by a much smaller group of militia all lined up for battle. The men in the militia were called *minutemen* because they could be ready in a minute to defend their country. Shots were fired and several patriots were killed. This was the beginning of the War for Independence. The first bullet fired is called "the shot heard round the world" because it began a war that would dramatically change the whole world.

The British marched on to Concord where they were met by a larger group of minutemen. These men held their ground, killing several of the "redcoats" (British uniforms were bright red). The British retreated toward Boston. As they marched back along the main road, they were attacked on every side by militiamen firing from behind rocks, trees, and buildings. About 250 British soldiers were killed or wounded on that long march. Blood had been shed on both sides; Britain and America were at war.

Bunker Hill. After Lexington and Concord, men came from all over the colonies to surround Boston. This people's army set up fortifications on a hill near the city called Breeds Hill. They had planned to build fortifications on Bunker Hill. The battle was named after that hill by mistake.

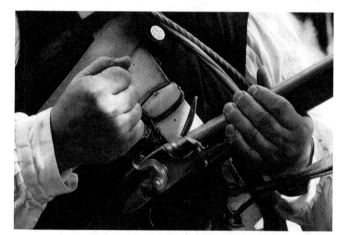

| "Hold fire 'till you can see the whites of their eyes!"

The British attacked the Americans on Breeds Hill on June 17, 1775. The British in their red uniforms marched straight up the hill toward the Americans. The Americans were ordered not to fire until they "could see the whites of their eyes." Thus, when the British were very close, the Americans opened fire and drove them back. The British came back up again, with the same result. Finally, the Americans ran out of gunpowder to fire their weapons and had to leave. Almost half the British soldiers were killed or wounded while the American losses were much lower. The British paid dearly for their victory. They should have been wise enough to take notice and consider carefully if they wanted to face more fighting like this.

Second Continental Congress. The Second Continental Congress met as planned in May of 1775. They heard about the army around Boston and decided to take charge of it. They chose George Washington as the commander-in-chief of the American army and sent him to Boston to take his post. They also sent one last petition to the king, hoping to end this war before it went any further.

The king refused to even see the petition and began his own preparations for war. He hired soldiers, called Hessians, from Germany to fight for the British in America. This upset the patriots even more. They could not believe the king would use foreign soldiers to fight against his own people!

Declaration of Independence. The American people finally decided that they were not going to get what they wanted from the British government. A man named Thomas Paine wrote a very important pamphlet called *Common Sense* in 1776. In it, he wrote that common sense required that the colonies be free and independent of Britain. Copies of the pamphlet were read by people all over the colonies and the people agreed with him. Because of that pamphlet, many Americans finally decided to fight, not for their rights as Englishmen, but for their freedom as Americans.

The Continental Congress began to debate whether they should declare independence in June of 1776. A committee was chosen to write a paper declaring independence and explaining the reasons for it. Thomas Jefferson, John Adams, and Benjamin Franklin were on the committee, but Jefferson did the writing. The paper he wrote is called

| The Declaration of Independence

the Declaration of Independence. Many strong words in it tell about how the rights of the Americans were ignored by the British government. An important part of it reads:

> **We hold these truths to be self evident: that all men are created equal; that they are endowed by their Creator with certain unalienable rights; that among these are life, liberty, and the pursuit of happiness;...**

Congress voted for independence on July 2, 1776. However, the Declaration of Independence was not accepted until two days later on July 4, 1776, which became the day Americans celebrate their nation's birthday. However, this was only a declaration, the Americans still had to win the war before they were truly free.

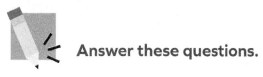

Answer these questions.

3.52   Where did the Revolutionary War begin? _____

3.53   What happened to the British soldiers marching back from Lexington and Concord?

_____

_____

3.54   Who was the famous rider that rode to warn the patriots at Lexington and Concord?

_____

3.55   What did General Gage hope to capture at Lexington and Concord?

_____

3.56   a. What was the name of the battle outside Boston when the British marched

straight up into the American fire and were driven back twice?

_____

b. Where was that battle fought? _____

3.57   a. What happened in Congress on July 2, 1776?_____

_____

b. on July 4, 1776? _____

_____

3.58   The militia fighters who could be ready to fight in 60 seconds were called what?

_____

3.59   What was the pamphlet by Thomas Paine that made Americans decide to fight for

independence? _____

3.60   Who wrote the Declaration of Independence?

_____

3.61   Who did the Second Continental Congress name as the commander in chief of the

American army? _____

3.62   Where did the Sons of Liberty put the signal to warn about the redcoats leaving

to attack Lexington and Concord? _____

3.63   a. What does it mean for a truth to be "self evident?" (Ask if you need help.)

_____

b. According to the Declaration of Independence, what is true of all men?

_____

c. "Unalienable rights" are ones that can not be taken away. List three of them.

_____

d. Who gave us unalienable rights? _____

🔄 **Before you take this last Self Test, you may want to do one or more of these self checks.**

1. _____ Read the objectives. See if you can do them.

2. _____ Restudy the material related to any objectives that you cannot do.

3. _____ Use the **SQ3R** study procedure to review the material:

a. **S**can the sections.

b. **Q**uestion yourself.

c. **R**ead to answer your questions.

d. **R**ecite the answers to yourself.

e. **R**eview areas you did not understand.

4. _____ Review all vocabulary, activities, and Self Tests, writing a correct answer for every wrong answer.

SELF TEST 3

Match these items (each answer, 2 points). Some answers will be used more than once.

3.01 _____ Revival in America, 1730s and '40s

3.02 _____ Ordered colonists not to settle west of the Appalachians

3.03 _____ Parliament said it could control the colonies any way it wanted

3.04 _____ Five people were killed after throwing things at British soldiers on guard duty

3.05 _____ Beginning of the War for Independence

3.06 _____ All of the events that changed the British colonies into the United States of America

3.07 _____ Accepted on July 4, 1776

3.08 _____ Paul Revere rode to warn the patriots there

3.09 _____ War that gave the British control of Canada and all of the land east of the Mississippi

3.010 _____ George Whitefield and Jonathan Edwards

3.011 _____ Colonists had to feed and house British soldiers

3.012 _____ Sons of Liberty refused to accept the tea because of the tax on it

3.013 _____ People had to buy stamps for all important papers

3.014 _____ Battle for Breeds Hill near Boston; British marched straight up and many of their men were killed or hurt

3.015 _____ Tax on goods from Britain: tea, paint, glass

a. American Revolution
b. Declaration of Independence
c. French and Indian War
d. Great Awakening
e. Proclamation of 1763
f. Stamp Act
g. Quartering Act
h. Townshend Acts
i. Intolerable Acts
j. Declaratory Act
k. Boston Tea Party
l. Boston Massacre
m. Lexington
n. Bunker Hill

3.016 _____ Closed Boston harbor, put the city under military rule, took away many of Massachusetts's freedoms

3.017 _____ "We hold these truths to be self evident: that all men are created equal…"

3.018 _____ The First Continental Congress met to discuss these laws

3.019 _____ The British began to enforce the trade laws after this

3.020 _____ British soldiers were attacked all along their retreat back to Boston

Choose the correct person from the list below (each answer, 2 points).

George Washington	William Pitt	William Penn	George Grenville
Samuel Adams	Thomas Jefferson	George III	Squanto
Pontiac			Roger Williams

3.021 _____ was a Boston patriot who strongly opposed the British.

3.022 _____ founded Rhode Island with complete freedom of religion.

3.023 _____ was a Quaker who started the colonies of Delaware and Pennsylvania.

3.024 _____ was the king of Britain during the Revolution.

3.025 _____ was the Prime Minister of Britain who passed the Stamp Act.

3.026 _____ wrote the Declaration of Independence.

3.027 _____ helped the Pilgrims at Plymouth to survive.

3.028 _____ led the British to victory in the French and Indian War.

3.029 _____ organized the Native Americans to drive the colonists out of the land west of the Appalachian Mountains after the French and Indian War.

3.030 _____ was the commander in chief of the American army during the Revolutionary War.

Answer these questions (each item, 3 points).

3.031 What was the first British colony in America? _____

3.032 What happened to General Braddock on his way to Fort Duquesne, during the French and Indian War? _____

_____

3.033 What did the colonists do to fight the Stamp Act, the Townshend Acts, and the Intolerable Acts that put pressure on British merchants? _____

3.034 Why did Americans not want to be tried in Admiralty Court? _____

_____

_____

3.035 What was the first Congress for the colonies that nine of them attended?

_____

3.036 What was the name of Thomas Paine's pamphlet that convinced many Americans to fight for independence? _____

3.037 What were the three parts of a colonial government?

a. _____   b. _____

c. _____

3.038 What was the purpose of the British trade laws? _____

_____

_____

Answer true or false (each answer, 2 points).

3.039 _____ The people of Britain had more freedom than the American colonists.

3.040 _____ Many American men learned how to use a gun because of the danger from Indians on the frontier.

3.041 _____ George Washington fought in the French and Indian War.

3.042 _____ Europeans explored the New World because they wanted to find a water route to Asia.

3.043 _____ Georgia was founded by Puritans looking for the freedom to worship God in their own way.

Teacher check: Initials _____

Score _____ Date _____

80 / 100

Before you take the LIFEPAC Test, you may want to do one or more of these self checks.

1. _____ Read the objectives. See if you can do them.
2. _____ Restudy the material related to any objectives that you cannot do.
3. _____ Use the **SQ3R** study procedure to review the material.
4. _____ Review activities, Self Tests, and LIFEPAC vocabulary words.
5. _____ Restudy areas of weakness indicated by the last Self Test.

NOTES